DISCARD

The First Americans

INDIANS OF THE NORTHEAST

Colin G. Calloway

Facts On File, Inc.

AN INFOBASE HOLDINGS COMPANY

About *The First Americans* Series:

This eight-volume series presents the rich and varied cultures of the many Native American tribes, placing each within its geographical and historical context. Each volume covers a different cultural area, providing an understanding of all the major North American Indian tribes in a systematic, region-by-region survey. The series emphasizes the contributions of Native Americans to American culture, illustrating their legacy in striking photographs within the text and in all-color photo essays.

Indians of the Northeast

Facts On File, Inc.
11 Penn Plaza
New York NY 10001

Library of Congress Cataloging-in-Publication Data

Calloway, Colin G. (Colin Gordon), 1953–
     Indians of the Northeast / Colin G. Calloway
       p.   cm. — The First Americans series
     Includes index.
     Summary: Describes the Native American tribes of the Northeast,
the Narraganset, the Abnaki, the Iroquois, and the Nanticoke, and
the influence on them of their early contact with Europeans.
     ISBN 0-8160-2389-1
     1. Indians of North America—Northeastern States—Juvenile literature.
[1. Indians of North America—Northeastern States.]
I. Title   II. Series.
E78.E2C34   1991
974' .00497—dc20   90–47448

Facts On File books are available at special discounts when purchased in bulk quantities for businesses, associations, institutions or sales promotions. Please call our Special Sales Department in New York at 212/967-8800 or 800/322-8755.

Design by Carmela Pereira
Jacket design by Donna Sinisgalli
Typography & composition by Tony Meisel

10 9 8 7 6 5 4 3

This book is printed on acid-free paper.
Manufactured in MEXICO.

▲ In the late 19th and early 20th centuries, as their traditional ways of life were disrupted, many Indians turned to making baskets for sale to tourists. This Winnebago basket maker was photographed near the Wisconsin Dells, a popular tourist site.

CONTENTS

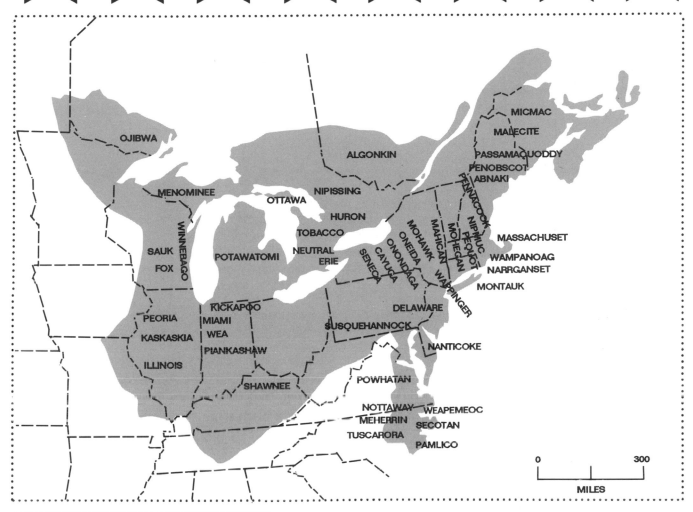

THE NORTHEAST CULTURE AREA

The approximate traditional tribal boundaries of the Northeast culture area are shown in the larger map, with modern state boundaries. The smaller map shows the culture area in relation to all of North America.

▲ A Chippewa chief named Rocky Boy wears an ornate costume decorated with embroidery in a photo from around 1880.

CHAPTER ONE

ROOTS

People have lived in the land that is now the Northeastern United States for thousands of years. Long before the United States was founded and long before Europeans ever set foot on the continent of North America, Indian people lived in this region of the country, cared for it, and left their mark on it. There were many different tribes, they spoke different languages, had many different customs, and sometimes fought against one another, but they shared similar ways of life in their woodland homes. Whether they lived in the Appalachian Mountains in the East, on the shores of the Great Lakes in the West, or in the rich valley of the Ohio River, the Indians of the Northeast inhabited a world of wooded hillsides, fertile valleys, clear lakes and brooks. They lived here in harmony with the natural world, enjoying the bounty and beauty of their world without destroying it.

Dozens of different Indian tribes lived in the region. No single tribe was typical of the entire Northeast, and some tribes who lived on the fringes of the area shared many characteristics with neighbors in the Subarctic, on the eastern Great Plains, or in the South. Most of the Northeastern tribes belonged to either the Algonquian or the Iroquoian language family. There were many language families in North America, but the Algonquian and Iroquoian were two of the largest. Members of a language family did not always speak the same language, but their languages were related and displayed similarities, as do, for example, Spanish and French. Members of the same language group were not always allies either, and sometimes bitter wars were fought as, for example, between the Huron and the Iroquois, both of whom belonged to the Iroquoian language family. Sometimes the various tribes of the Algonquian language family are referred to jointly as Algonquians, and those of the Iroquois language family as Iroquoians, but these terms should not be confused with names for any particular tribes.

The Indian tribes of New England and the Maritime Provinces of eastern Canada were Algonquian speakers. In Nova Scotia lived the Micmac, who had close ties with the Malecite and Passamaquoddy of northern Maine. Elsewhere in Maine the Penobscot, Kennebec, and other tribes were known collectively as the eastern Abnaki. The western Abnaki lived in New Hampshire and Vermont and included the Pigwacket, Pennacook, Sokoki, and Missisquois. Massachusetts was home to several Indian

tribes, including the Massachuset, the Wampanoag, and the Nipmuc. The Pequot and Mohegan lived in neighboring Connecticut, while the Narraganset inhabited Rhode Island.

The Hudson Valley, which forms New England's western border, was home to several Indian groups, among whom the Mahican were important. To the south of the New England tribes and the Mahican, the Lenape or Delaware Indians lived in what is now New Jersey and eastern Pennsylvania. In time the Delaware would be pushed west into Ohio by white settlers. There, they would live close to the Shawnee, who regarded Ohio as their original homeland but who went through many migrations in the course of their history. Other neighbors of the Delaware Indians included the Susquehannock in Pennsylvania, the Nanticoke in Maryland, and many smaller tribes.

Several powerful tribes of the Iroquoian language family occupied New York State. In the east, close to the Mahican, were the Mohawk. To their west lived the Oneida Indians; west of the Oneida in the Finger Lakes region were the Onondaga. The Cayuga lived to the west of the Onondaga, and the powerful Seneca occupied the western portion of the state. In time these five tribes became allied and formed the Iroquois Confederacy. Other Iroquoian people, who did not join the confederacy and sometimes fought against it, lived around the eastern Great Lakes. The Erie and Neutral lived on the shores of Lake Erie; the Huron lived on the north side of Lake Ontario, in what is today Ontario, Canada.

Around the western Great Lakes lived the Ottawa or Odawa, the Potawatomi, the Sauk and Fox, the Chippewa or Ojibwa (today many Ojibwa prefer to call themselves by their original Algonquin name, Anishinabe), and the Menominee. All these tribes were members of the Algonquian language family. The Winnebago, who lived in Wisconsin, belonged to a different language family, known as the Siouan. South of the Great Lakes region were the villages of the Miami in Ohio and Indiana, and the Illinois in the state of the same name. North of the Great Lakes, from Hudson Bay to the Great Plains, lived the Cree Indians of Canada.

Many of the Indian tribes of the Northeast moved about during their history as pressure from white settlers and other forces pushed them out of their homelands. Maps that show Indian tribes living in one place for all time can be very misleading to us today.

THE FIRST AMERICANS

All people try to find explanations for why the world is the way it is and how they come to be where they are. The people who have lived in the Northeast are no exception. Archaeologists— scientists who study the objects and remains of the past—and most other scholars agree that the first people to inhabit North America came from Asia. Today, Asia and North America are separated by a shallow channel of water known as the Bering Strait, but, many thousands of years ago, the earth was in the grip of ice ages for long periods. Because most of the water on earth freezes during an ice age, the water level of the world's oceans was much lower. The floor of the Bering Strait was exposed and it was possible to walk from Siberia to Alaska. This land bridge was open most recently several times between about 25,000 and 8,000 B.C. Archaeologists have pieced together a picture of how people moved from one continent to another. Slowly, over many generations, families of hunters following game drifted across the land bridge. They did not think they were migrating to a new world; they just kept moving where the hunting was best. Gradually, they began to move south into the heart of the North American continent. In time, the descendants of these very first Americans migrated and settled in every corner of the country. As the ice cap melted, some came to the area of the present Northeastern United States. When water covered the Bering Strait, America became separated from the Old World until Europeans began to venture across the Atlantic in ships thousands of years later.

THE WORLD ON A TURTLE'S BACK

Many Indian people tell a very different story of how the world came to be. They believe that they have lived in North America since time began. One Indian chief, a Miami warrior named Little Turtle, who lived in the 18th century, said that if the native people in Siberia and North America looked alike, that did not prove that Indians came from Asia. It might mean that the Asian people migrated to that continent from North America! Creation stories among the Northeastern Indians vary from tribe to tribe, but most recount how the world they live in was created on the back of a great sea turtle.

Among the Haudenosaunee, the Iroquois of

THE TRIBES AND LANGUAGE GROUPS OF THE NORTHEAST

The following is a list of the major Northeast tribes organized by language family.

ALGONQUIAN FAMILY

Abnaki	Mohegan	Sauk
Algonkin	Narraganset	Fox
Penobscot	Montauk	Shawnee
Pennacook	Mahican	Delaware (Lenape)
Passamaquoddy	Chippewa (Ojibwa)	Illinois
Micmac	Cree	Nanticoke
Malecite	Kickapoo	Powhatan
Massachuset	Ottawa	Wappinger
Wampanoag	Potawatomi	Peoria
Nipmuc	Menominee	Secotan
Pequot	Miami	

IROQUOIAN FAMILY

Mohawk	Seneca	Neutral
Oneida	Tuscarora	Erie
Onondaga	Huron (Wyandot)	Susquehannock
Cayuga		

SIOUAN FAMILY
Winnebago

New York State, storytellers say that long ago there was no earth, only the sky and the ocean. Long before there were human beings there were Sky People. The Sky Chief had a young wife called Aataentsic or Sky Woman, and they were going to have a baby. But one day, Sky Woman fell through a hole in the sky. She tried to hold on to something to prevent her from falling, but the roots and plants she grabbed came away in her hands and she plunged down toward the ocean below. But as Sky Woman fell, the birds flew underneath her to support her with their wings and broke her fall. When she reached the water, they laid her gently on the back of Turtle.

Sky Woman was afraid she would die, but the creatures of the sea came to her and asked what they could do to help. Sky Woman told them that if they could find some soil, she would plant the roots caught between her fingers. One after another, the animals dived deep into the cold waters but none were able to bring her any earth. Many died trying. Finally Muskrat said he would try. He dived into the ocean and disappeared. Sky Woman and the other animals waited anxiously, but Muskrat did not return. Finally, he floated to the surface, with a tiny clump of earth clutched in his paw.

Sky Woman took the clump of soil and placed it in the middle of Turtle's back. Then she walked around it in a circle, moving in the same direction that the sun travels. The earth began to grow and she planted the roots in it, and grass and trees began to grow. To keep things growing, Sky Woman continued to walk in a circle around the earth, in the same direction as the sun goes.

In time, Sky Woman gave birth to a baby girl. When the girl became a woman, the daughter gave birth to twins. One of the twins was good, the other was evil. The Good Twin was born first, but the Evil Twin was in a hurry to be born and pushed his way through his mother's side and killed her. Sky Woman buried her daughter and from her grave grew the plants that the people still use: corn, beans, and squash, known as the Three Sisters; tobacco, which the people use in sacred ceremonies; and medicinal plants to cure the sick.

The twins grew to manhood and each created things themselves. The Good Twin made good things, such as animals, plants, berries, and rivers; the Evil Twin made bad things such as poisonous plants, thorns, diseases, and monsters. Finally the Good Twin created human beings. The twins were always fighting, and the world

they made was a mixture of good and evil. But everything was in balance. Different animals and plants had different purposes. Medicinal plants cured sickness. Pain existed alongside pleasure; there was joy as well as sorrow. The people who lived in the world had a special place in it but they also had a responsibility to look after it, as did all the creatures. This is the way the world was made in the beginning, and this is how it was supposed to be for all time if the world was to survive. To the Haudenosaunee, all of North America has always been known as Turtle Island.

Other Northeastern tribes tell similar stories to explain how the world came to be. The creation legend of the Chippewa and Ottawa people who live around the western Great Lakes tells that the Great Spirit had a dream in which he saw a world of balance and harmony. When he awoke he decided to create that world. He made rock, fire, wind, and water first, and from them he made the sun, the moon, the earth, and the stars, and breathed a spirit into them. Next he made plants, flowers, and trees, then animals, birds, reptiles, and fish, and he gave each one its own character and special powers. Last of all he made human beings—the Anishinabe ("first people")—and gave them a special gift: the power to dream. Because all the creatures had their own different qualities, they all lived together in harmony.

But a great flood disrupted the world's harmony. The animals called out to Sky Woman to come down and help them. Sky Woman descended from the skies and came to rest on the back of the Great Turtle. She asked for some earth and Muskrat brought it. Sky Woman spread the earth around the Great Turtle's back and breathed life into it. The earth grew and formed an island, which the people called The Place of the Great Turtle's Back. Today Americans call it the Island of Michillimackinac, and it is located where Lake Michigan and Lake Huron meet. At this place Sky Woman gave birth to a boy and girl and they in turn had children. The cycle of life began anew and Sky Woman returned to her home in the sky.

The world of the Lenape or Delaware began when Kishelemukong, the Creator, brought up a giant turtle from the depths of the ocean. The turtle grew into a great island that became North America. The first men and women sprouted from a tree growing on the turtle's back. Kishelemukong then made the sun, the moon, place, he decided to stay there forever. He climbed on to a rock in the middle of the lake and turned himself into a stone, which is now called Rock Dunder or the Guardian's Rock. Abnaki regard Rock Dunder as a sacred place even to this day.

Northeastern Indians revere the turtle as a special creature and attach great importance to the symbol of the turtle in art and ceremony. Their creation stories show that humans exist due to the efforts of other beings and that they must be grateful to the animals who gave their lives so that humans could live. They express understanding of the balance and respect for life that is needed to keep the world. Northeastern Indian people have always recalled these important principles in their customs, art, and dances and have always taught their children that a special link exists between the people and the land, between humans and animals.

Many stories illustrate the delicate balance that exists between all the creatures of the world and that all things were created for a purpose. The stories of creation and how the world came to be the way it was were preserved in memory by the old people of the tribe, and they were told and retold on countless winter evenings as sleepy-eyed children huddled around warm fires in the lodges of the village. Through their stories the children learned that human beings had a special place on the back of the Great Turtle, but that they must not think that they knew better than their Creator nor try to change things or in-

▲ The creation stories of many Northeastern Indian tribes tell how the world grew up on the back of a giant sea turtle. Here, the Iroquois Tree of Peace is shown resting on Turtle's back in a clay sculpture by Oneida Diane Schenandoah.

and the heavens, the plants and animals, and the four directions and winds that caused the seasons to change.

The Abnaki of Vermont believed that the world was created by Tabaldak, the Creator. After he had finished making human beings, Tabaldak brushed the dust from his hands, and Gluskab, a traditional hero, formed himself out of the dust. Tabaldak gave Gluskab the power to make the world a good place for the Abnaki to live, but in some stories Gluskab had a twin brother, who went around doing evil. Abnaki also tell the story of Odzihozo, "the Man Who Made Himself," and how he formed the hills and valleys of their homeland by dragging himself around before he had legs, pushing up piles of earth with his hands. Finally he made Lake Champlain and, seeing it was the most beautiful

▼ A rattle made from the shell of a snapping turtle. Turtle shell rattles, filled with pebbles or cherry pits, were used in the curing rituals of the Iroquois False Face societies and in other festivals and ceremonies.

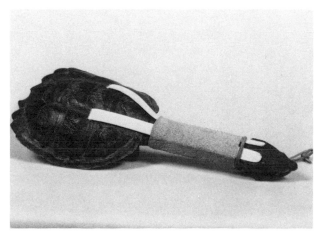

THE MAKING OF NIGHT AND DAY

Besides explaining how the world was created, Indian stories told why things were the way they were, why animals had certain characteristics, and how animals played a role in making the world. This tale comes from the Iroquois people of New York.

Once upon a time all the animals got together and chose the porcupine as their leader. Soon after his appointment the porcupine called them all together and asked them whether they wanted to have night and darkness all the time, or daylight and sunshine. This was a very important question and a violent discussion arose. Some wanted daylight and sun; others preferred continual night.

The chipmunk wished for night and day, weeks and months, and night to be separate from the day, so he began singing for light to come. Meanwhile the bear began singing that night was best and that they must have darkness.

While the chipmunk was singing, the day began to dawn. Then the other party saw that the chipmunk was prevailing and were very angry; and their leader, the bear, chased the chipmunk, who managed to escape uninjured, the huge paw of the bear simply grazing his back as he entered his hole in a hollow tree, leaving its black imprint, which the chipmunk has ever since retained. But night and day have ever continued to alternate.

Adapted from *Tales of the North American Indians*, selected and edited by Stith Thompson, Bloomington: Indiana University Press, 1929, p. 39–40.

▲ Pipes played an important role in intertribal trade and diplomacy, and Iroquois men excelled in the making of pipes. This eagle pipe is carved from catlinite (a soft stone) and wood.

terfere with nature. They learned they had to look after the land, treat the animals with respect, and use the plants and other resources with care. If they forgot to do these things they would destroy the harmony and balance that was given to the world at its creation.

THE ANCIENT ONES

By investigating thousands of sites, large and small, throughout Northeastern North America, archaeologists have been able to learn something of how ancient peoples lived long before Europeans came here. They have unearthed arrowheads, fragments of pottery, bones, evidence of campfires, and remnants of shelters. There is still disagreement about how long ago human beings first inhabited the Northeast. Estimates of when the first humans set foot in North America vary widely. Some archaeologists say Indians were here as much as 40,000 years ago; others disagree. New evidence keeps turning up that causes people to think that humans may have occupied the continent much earlier than was once thought, and we must remember that many Indian people believe they have been here since the beginning of time. Indian peoples were certainly living in the Northeastern part of the United States over 10,000 years ago, perhaps as much as 20,000 years ago.

Archaeologists divide the history of North America before European contact into three different periods:

▶ The Paleo-Indian period, from roughly

25,000 years ago to about 10,000 years ago.
▶ The Archaic period, between 10,000 years ago and 3,000 years ago.
▶ The Woodland period, from about 3,000 years ago to around A.D. 1500

From 1500 to the present is called the Contact period, since after 1500 the Indians of the Northeast were in constant contact with Europeans.

The people whom archaeologists and anthropologists call Paleo-Indians began to make the Northeast their home toward the end of the last ice age. Paleo-Indians lived mainly by hunting big game. Some of the animals they hunted were huge and are now extinct, such as the mammoth and the mastodon. Others, like the caribou and musk ox, now live far to the north in much colder climates. As the ice receded and the climate in the Northeastern United States became warmer and wetter, new plants and forests grew up, inhabited by smaller animals like deer. The Northeast became a much more hospitable place to live and a new way of life evolved, which archaeologists call the Archaic era.

Archaic people hunted deer, elk, bear, small mammals, fish, geese, and ducks. They also gathered wild plant foods such as nuts, berries, and roots. They moved from place to place as the seasons changed, hunting and gathering where the food resources were richest. Often they lived on the coast, a lake shore, or the bank of a river where they could add fish and birds to the food they obtained by hunting and gathering. They developed better stone tools than the Paleo-Indians had made. For example, they learned to chop down trees and hollow out dugout canoes. They built themselves shelters of wood and brush in-

▼ Ceremonial pipes such as this one were often interred in the Native American burial mounds found throughout the Northeastern United States.

WORDS AND PLACE NAMES

The Algonquian and Iroquian languages provide us with many words and names we use today. There are thousands of Indian names used for towns, counties, rivers, and lakes throughout the Northeast. The following list is a small sample.

WORDS

moose	powwow
raccoon	moccasin
caribou	opossum
skunk	woodchuck
chipmunk	toboggan
succotash	

PLACE NAMES

Agawam (Mass.)	Ottawa (Ontario, Ohio)
Pigwacket (Maine)	Chillicothe (Ohio)
Penobscot (Maine)	Piqua (Ohio)
Pawtucket (R.I., Mass., Conn.)	Michigan
Niagara (N.Y.)	Illinois
Nashua (Mass., N.H.)	Kankakee (Ill., Ind.)
Nantucket (Mass.)	Oswegatchie (N.Y.)
Massachusetts	Miami (Ohio)
Chappaquiddick (Mass.)	Canajoharie (N.Y.)
Androscoggin (Maine, N.H.)	Narragansett (R.I.)
Genesee (N.Y.)	Missisquoi (Vt.)
Allegheny (N.Y., Penn.)	Kennebec (Maine)
Erie (Penn.)	Sandusky (Ohio)
Saginaw (Mich.)	Susquehanna (N.Y., Penn.)
Canandaigua (N.Y.)	Ogunquit (Maine)
Tonawanda (N.Y.)	Winnipesaukee (N.H.)
Chenango (N.Y.)	Pennacook (N.H.)
Chicago (Ill.)	Merrimack (N.H.)
Cayuga (N.Y., Ohio)	Connecticut
Oneonta (N.Y.)	

▲ Aerial view of the Great Serpent Mound, in Adams County, Ohio. This is the world's largest serpent effigy. Scholars believe Indians of the Adena culture built the mound for ritual use between 1,300 and 3,000 years ago. The oval may represent an egg or the snake's open mouth.

stead of living in caves, and they lived together in larger groups. These trends continued into the Woodland period. During that era, Indian peoples in Northeastern North America learned how to make pottery, to hunt with bows and arrows, and to grow crops.

Before pottery, Indian people used baskets, wooden bowls, and vessels carved in soft stone to store and cook their food. The art of making fired clay pottery spread from the south, and Indian women soon found they could make much better vessels for cooking and storing food. They gathered clay from riverbanks, broke it up and wet it, kneaded it, formed the shape of pot they wanted, and then fired it to make it hard.

Indian men learned to make and use bows and arrows. They fashioned smaller points to use as arrowheads and found that they could stalk and strike their prey from a greater distance, and in greater safety, by using a bow and arrow instead of a spear.

Northeastern Indians gathered plants in the Archaic period, but by the Woodland period, they had developed a system of agriculture based on new crops of corn, beans, and squash, with many other plants as supplements. Corn, squash, and beans provided a nutritious food supply that was much more reliable than hunting, gathering, and fishing. Indians continued to hunt and fish, and in some areas like northern New England, where the climate was harsh and uncertain, cultivated crops never became as important as they did farther south. But elsewhere, Indians began

to spend more months of the year living in settled villages while the women planted, tended, and harvested the crops. The new source of food meant that Indians did not have to be on the move all the time and they could live together in larger numbers than ever before.

In some areas, Indians built impressive towns and religious structures. In the Ohio Valley, people the archaeologists call Adena and Hopewell erected elaborate burial mounds, some of which can still be seen today. The Adena people built the great Serpent Mound in Adams County, Ohio, sometime between 1,300 and 3,000 years ago. The mound is a quarter of a mile long and five feet high, and it was originally much higher. Archaeologists have puzzled over its exact age and purpose for generations, but the mound certainly served some ritual purpose. The Adena people filled the graves of important people with things they valued in life, and archaeologists have found skillfully carved figures and stone pipes.

After the Adena people, another group of people continued the practice of building mounds. They are known as the Hopewell, after a site in Ohio that archaeologists excavated in the 19th century. Some of the Hopewell burial mounds in Ohio are up to three miles long and

▲ This 19th-century woodcut shows an Indian village. Though the huts resemble the grass huts of southeastern Indians, the palisade (a fence made of pointed wooden stakes) was a common feature of Indian villages in the Northeast.

contained great wealth in goods that were buried alongside leaders. Beads, pipes, copper jewelry, knives, cloth, carved animal figures, and a variety of ornaments have been uncovered from these burial mounds.

By the end of the Woodland period, many Northeastern Indian people lived in settled villages and had developed separate customs and cultures. But they also traded extensively. When times were hard, they would trade for food; at other times they might trade for less essential items. Trade items from as far away as the Rocky Mountains and the Gulf of Mexico found their way into the Northeast, and the influence of Indian peoples living in the south came to be seen in the art, pottery, and agriculture of Northeastern Indians. The tribes of the Northeast had an ancient past long before Europeans came to America and called it the New World. In the next chapter we will see how these tribes lived.

LIVING ON THE LAND

THE BEAUTY OF THE NORTHEAST

▼ Lake Champlain was the border between the homelands of the Iroquois in New York and the Abnaki in Vermont. It was also the site of many Abnaki legends and creation stories.

▼ The forest homelands of the Indians of northern New England produced rich displays of foliage in the autumn months. The forest was the home of deer and turkey, and the source of fruits, nuts, and other important foods.

▶ The White River in Vermont is typical of the relatively shallow, rapids-filled rivers of the Northeast. The Abnaki and their neighbors inhabited a world of mountains, forests, and streams that provided plentiful food supply.

PLANTS OF IMPORTANCE

◀ Paper birch trees, common throughout the cool, moist woodlands of the Northeast, provided the Indian inhabitants with the raw material for building canoes and for making a variety of containers and utensils.

▼ Indian women gathered a wide variety of wild plants to add to their families' diet. Blueberries and other berries were abundant.

ANIMALS OF IMPORTANCE

▶ Northeastern Indians used the quills of the porcupine to fashion beautiful decoration for clothes, birch-bark boxes, and jewelry. The quills were cleaned, dyed, and worked into colorful patterns. In later years, glass beads imported from Europe often replaced quillwork as a form of decoration.

◀ Wild turkeys are very wary and hard to hunt, but they were a favorite food of the Native Americans in the Northeast.

◀ The white-tailed deer was an essential resource for Indian people throughout the Northeastern United States. Deer provided woodland Indians with food and clothing, thongs, thread and string made from sinews, tools made from bones and antlers, and rattles from hooves.

▼ In the spring and fall, migrating Canada geese pass over the Northeast in great numbers. They were eagerly hunted by the Indians of the region.

▲ In the creation stories of the Iroquois and other Northeastern Indian peoples, the muskrat played a crucial role, diving to the bottom of the ocean and bringing up the first earth to be spread on the back of the turtle.

CHAPTER TWO

LIVING

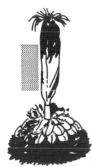

n the thousands of years during which they inhabited the Northeastern United States, Indians developed ways of life that suited them well and worked effectively for countless generations. Northeastern Indian tribes usually consisted of several villages, bands, and clans, loosely united by language, kinship, and shared interests. Indian communities varied in size: villages normally numbered several hundred people but they sometimes were as large as a few thousand, and they often changed in size as people came and went with the seasons. Sometimes whole villages broke up as small groups dispersed to go hunting, and then reassembled later in the year to gather for winter ceremonies or for spring planting.

SOCIAL ORGANIZATION

The family was the core of Northeastern Indian life. An Indian family included not only parents and children, as in a modern American family, but also grandparents, aunts, uncles, cousins, and in-laws. There was often a much closer bond between these relatives than in modern extended families. The members of a family band lived close together and sometimes lived under the

same roof. A Northeastern Indian baby was born into a world surrounded by relatives. Brothers, sisters, aunts, uncles, grandparents, and cousins, as well as parents, all took a hand in the child's welfare and upbringing. When a mother went about her daily tasks or worked in the fields with the other women, she carried the baby with her in a cradleboard and hung the board from a tree branch so the child could be close by and see all that was going on. Children took part in all aspects of family life and were expected to behave in a way that would be helpful to the others. Above all, young people were taught to respect their elders, and grandmothers were treated with special regard.

As well as being part of a family, a Northeastern Indian was also a member of a clan. Clans were groups of related people who traced their descent to a common ancestor. Each clan had as its name and symbol a certain animal. The Delaware had Wolf, Turkey, and Turtle clans; the Mohawk had Turtle, Wolf, and Bear; others had Heron, Snipe, Beaver, Elk, Deer, and Hawk. Many tribes were matrilineal; that is, they traced descent on the mother's side of the family. In these tribes, a person inherited clan membership at birth through the mother. A boy whose mother was a member of the Bear clan would himself be a member of the Bear clan. When he grew up he was not allowed to marry someone from his own clan so he would take a wife from another clan, for example the Turtle clan. His sons and daughters would then become members of the Turtle clan. A person who traveled from his home village to another village would be welcomed by members of the same clan. Clans often had special responsibilities and there were clan chiefs, just as there were leaders of the family bands.

When a couple married, the husband often moved from his own family to live with or near his wife's family. The women named and raised the children and were responsible for household affairs. Indians were affectionate parents and rarely disciplined their children with corporal punishment or harsh words. Instead, when children misbehaved their parents would sometimes shame them into acting better. Early Europeans thought the Indians let their children run wild and did nothing to educate them, but in fact Indian children received valuable education. Their elders taught them the skills they needed, told them the ancient stories that explained the way things were, and instilled in them the value of living in harmony with the rest of the community and the natural world. Young girls were taught in the traditional ways of women so they would become good wives and mothers when they grew up. Young boys were taught to be hunters and warriors so they could provide for and protect their families when they grew up. Many of the games that woodland Indian children played helped to prepare them for their roles in later life. Girls played with corn-husk and carved wooden dolls; boys competed to excel in foot races or games of skill, agility, and strength. A favorite game in winter was snowsnakes, in which players skimmed long wooden sticks, carved to resemble snakes, along the ice. Adults too participated in games like lacrosse, from which our modern sport is copied, and enjoyed gambling with bone dice.

POLITICAL STRUCTURE

When Europeans arrived in Northeastern America they discovered Indian people living very happily without powerful leaders, without bodies who passed legislation that controlled the whole society, and without agencies to enforce the laws. They often said the Indians had no real government. On the contrary, Indians governed themselves through a variety of relationships and obligations that functioned to serve the best in-

▲ Indian girls played with carved wooden dolls or with corn-husk dolls such as this one, which is dressed in traditional Iroquois cloth clothing. The blank face of the doll shows the corn husks used to make the body.

terests of the whole community.

Indian leaders did not rule. They offered advice, tried to resolve disputes, and put into practice the wishes of their people. Northeastern Indians made decisions, not by majority vote as happens in our society, but by reaching consensus. This meant that everyone had a chance to speak on the issue in question and a final decision would be made only when everyone agreed to support it. This was a time-consuming process but it worked well: by the time a decision was reached everyone had agreed on it, so no one could complain about it afterward.

An Indian leader (usually a man but it might also be a woman) was responsible for the welfare of his relatives. He was usually chosen as leader because of his skill as a hunter, his courage as a warrior, or his power as a speaker. But he might also be a leader because of his ability to cure the

◄ The Onondaga chief Tadodaho, or Atotarho, was said to have twisted snakes in his hair and to use supernatural powers against his enemies. Although he at first opposed Hiawatha and Deganawidah, Tadodaho eventually came around to accepting their plan for a league of peace among the Iroquois tribes. This modern soapstone carving was made in 1980 by Cleveland Sandy, a Cayuga.

THE GREAT LAW OF PEACE

Two great leaders, Deganawidah (a Huron) and Hiawatha (an Onondaga), persuaded many tribes in the Northeast to stop fighting with each other and live in harmony instead. According to legend, Hiawatha told the chiefs about the Great Law of Peace:

He [The Peacemaker] instructed the chiefs to regard courage, patience, and honesty as virtues most requisite to their responsibilities; and he urged them to think not so much of present advantage as of the future welfare of their people.

"When you administer the Law," he said, "your skins must be seven thumbs thick. Then the magic darts of your enemies will not penetrate, even if they prod you with their points.

"This is to be of strong mind, O chiefs: Carry no anger and hold no grudges. Think of continuing generations of our families, think of our grandchildren and of those yet unborn, whose faces are coming from beneath the ground."

Paul A. Wallace, *The White Roots of Peace*, Saranac Lake, N.Y.: Chauncy Press, 1986, p. 43.

sick, or because of some other special attribute that suggested that he had the support of strong spirit forces. The leader also had to be generous (often giving away all he had to the less fortunate), wise, and respected as a person. Chiefs led by good example and depended upon the support of their followers. A chief who acted unwisely, behaved rashly, or seemed to bring bad luck to his people would soon lose prestige. Women often occupied important political positions. Among the Iroquois, the clan mothers chose the council chiefs and could remove them from office.

There were no police, no jails, and no courts. People were expected to behave in a way that benefited the whole community, not just to look out for their own interests. The family and the community were the core of a person's life and no one wanted to lose their good opinion by acting in a selfish or disruptive manner.

The families, bands, and clans that made up a tribe enjoyed a lot of independence. If a family band disagreed with what the tribe as a whole was doing, they might move away from the rest of the tribe. In turn, individuals or groups from other tribes might be adopted, and they would take on the identity of the family or clan that took them in.

There was even less unity among different tribes. Tribes sometimes fought each other. Nevertheless, several important and powerful confederacies developed in the Northeast as tribes

THE HURON GROW CORN

Frenchman Gabriel Sagard recorded this description of Huron agriculture early in the 17th century:

They cut down the trees at the height of two or three feet from the ground, then they strip off all the branches, which they burn at the foot of these trees to make them die, and with the passage of time they remove the roots; then the women clear the land between the trees and dig a place or round holes at intervals of a pace, in which they sow nine or ten grains of maize that they have first selected, sorted, and soaked several days in water; they continue this until they have enough for two or three years' provisions, either for fear of having a bad year or for trade with other nations for peltries or things of which they need; every year they sow their corn in the same places, which they till with little wooden shovels, made in the form of an ear, which have a handle at the end; the rest of the ground is not worked, only cleaned of weeds; they take so much care to keep all clean that the fields appear to be roads; and that was the reason why going alone sometimes from one village to another I usually lost my way in these cornfields, more than in the prairies and forests.

W. Vernon Kinietz, *The Indians of the Western Great Lakes, 1615–1760,* University of Michigan Press, Ann Arbor Paperbacks, 1965, p. 16.

recognized that unity and strength were in the best interests of all. Some of these confederacies grew up in response to European invasion and the pressures of white settlers, but some were much older.

THE IROQUOIS CONFEDERACY

The most famous Indian confederacy in the Northeast, and in North America as a whole, was the Iroquois Confederacy, which survives today. According to tradition, the confederacy was formed long ago in a time of trouble and strife for the Iroquois people. There was constant warfare between the tribes, and as warriors fought to revenge the death of their relatives an endless cycle of killing resulted. Two men had the vision to try to end the fighting and begin a new era of peace. One was Deganawidah, a wandering Huron; the other was an Onondaga named Hiawatha or Hayenwatha. They proposed forming a confederation or a family of tribes that would live together in a league of peace. Each tribe that agreed to stop fighting and unite with the others would become a member of the confederacy. The clan chiefs would become the chiefs of the confederacy, but the clans and tribes would not lose their independence.

Together, Deganawidah and Hiawatha carried their message through the woodlands. One by one, the tribes agreed to observe the Great Law of Peace. The Mohawk were the first to accept the idea, and they sent messengers to the Oneida, who agreed to make peace. The strongest opposition to Hiawatha and Deganawidah came from an Onondaga chief called Tadodaha or Atotarho. He was said to be fierce and cruel, with twisted snakes in his hair, and he used spiritual powers against his enemies. But eventually even Tadodaha was persuaded to agree to the idea. The Cayuga and Seneca also joined the confederacy.

The tribes of this Iroquois Confederacy, often called the League of the Five Nations, agreed to stop fighting among themselves and unite in common defense. They kept control of their own affairs at the local level, but united in dealing with other tribes and later with foreign powers. Like the longhouses in which the Iroquois lived, the league could be extended to accommodate other people who wished to join. Early in the 18th century, the Tuscarora, who had been driven from their homes in the Carolinas, migrated north and joined the confederacy, which then became known as the Six Nations.

The Mohawk, who defended the eastern borders of the Iroquois homeland, were called the Keepers of the Eastern Door. The Seneca in the west were Keepers of the Western Door. The Confederacy's meeting place or council fire was located in Onondaga territory near present-day Syracuse, New York, at the center of Iroquois country. Each tribe sent chiefs to the great council at Onondaga, which met at least once a year, usually in the late summer or fall. There were 50 council chiefs, although other people could also attend council meetings. After lengthy deliberation, the council reached decisions by consensus. Each of the five tribes had a single vote so that they were all equal. The members of the league addressed each other as brothers and spoke of the league as a bundle of arrows, symbolizing the strength that came from being united; single arrows could be snapped easily but a bundle was hard to break.

The Iroquois Confederacy worked well for many years, although it was not always able to extend the message of peace to other tribes. Anthropologists and other scholars have long been fascinated by the Confederacy and its workings. Many people believe that the Iroquois form of government provided the founding fathers with a model when they drew up the Constitution of the United States.

Other tribes also united into confederacies, although these were not as old nor as famous as that of the Iroquois. The Micmac, Maliseet, Passamaquoddy, and the various Abnaki tribes developed a loose alliance known as the Wabnaki Confederacy. The Chippewa, Ottawa and Potawatomi formed their own alliance known as the Three Fires. The Illinois Confederacy contained several small tribes, such as the Kaskaskia, Michigamiea, and Peoria. The Wappinger Confederacy, relatives of the Delaware, was made up of Indian villages in Connecticut and eastern New York. Indian peoples who migrated to Canada formed an alliance called the Seven Nations of Canada. As the United States pushed westward into Ohio and Indiana, Indian tribes in that area also formed confederacies to defend their homelands. One of the most famous was led by the Shawnee chief, Tecumseh.

FOOD AND SUBSISTENCE

Northeastern Indians lived in an area that was rich in natural resources. Forests of birch, maple,

▲ Chack-scheb-nee-nick-ah, or Young Eagle, a Winnebago man photographed in 1904. The Winnebago
originated in Wisconsin but during the course of their
history many migrated as far west as Nebraska, where
they adopted some of the ways of the Plains Indians.

oak, beech, pine, spruce, and fir trees provided bark for houses and canoes, wood for fuel and tools, and roots and splints for baskets. Deer, beaver, otter, raccoon, rabbits, and in northern regions, moose, provided a variety of food and hides for clothing. Lakes, rivers, and streams were filled with fish. For coastal tribes, the seashore offered shellfish, fish, geese, and ducks, and some fishermen ventured far from shore to take sturgeon, swordfish, seals, and even whales. Fertile valleys produced extensive crops of corn, beans, and squash. Nuts, blueberries, raspberries, and strawberries grew wild, and Indian women collected them to add to the larder. Certain plants had medicinal properties and could be used to cure ailments and injuries.

Life revolved around the seasons as Indian people utilized different sources of food and men and women performed different tasks in securing food for their families. The division of labor between men and women, mutually supportive, ensured the smooth running of village life.

In the spring, Indians gathered for fishing near waterfalls and rapids. The men netted and speared shad, salmon, and other fish as they struggled upriver to spawn, but this was also a time for visiting and ceremonies after the long winter. Much of the spring catch was smoked for future use but fishing was a year-round activity, using hook and line, traps, weirs, and ice-fishing in the winter. The early spring was also the time for collecting sap from maple trees. The women tapped the maple trees by inserting grooved pieces of wood, gathered the sap in birch-bark containers and boiled it to make maple sugar.

Spring was also the time for planting crops. Corn, beans, and squash were the most important crops. Many tribes called these the Three Sisters and revered them as providing the staple diet for the people. Most tribes had several varieties of corn including popcorn. But these were not the only crops; pumpkins, sunflowers, and tobacco were also common. The men cleared the fields by cutting and burning the trees and brush, and the women planted and cared for the crops, working the soil with hoes. They planted kernels of pre-soaked corn in hills, two or three feet apart. After the corn began to grow, they also planted beans in the hills. When the soil became exhausted after several harvests, Indians moved their villages and cleared and planted new fields.

In the summer, the women were kept busy tending the crops in the clearings around the village and gathering berries, while the men went

▲ This Winnebago bandolier pouch or shoulder bag shows the mixture of native designs and European materials. The pouch is made of cloth, decorated with woolen tassels, and has a total of 88,240 colored beads.

hunting. Summer was also a time for travel, to visit friends, trade with neighboring tribes, or raid one's enemies.

In the fall the women harvested and dried the crops while the men hunted for deer, or even bear. Hunters sometimes would be gone for many days, stalking deer with bows and arrows, but when they returned home to the village, the women took over and butchered the meat. They often cut it into long strips and smoked it, to preserve it for food in winter. They also stretched the skins on a frame, scraped them clean, tanned them to make them supple, and smoked them to make leather.

Besides cultivated crops, most tribes gathered wild plant foods, such as berries, fruit, and roots. Many Indian tribes harvested wild rice. Wild rice grows in shallow lakes, ponds, and swampy areas from the Atlantic coast to the Mississippi

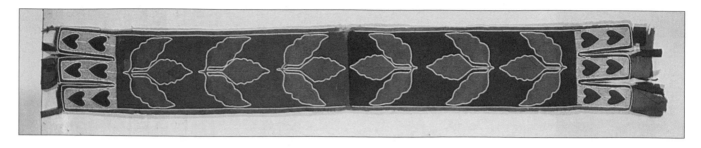

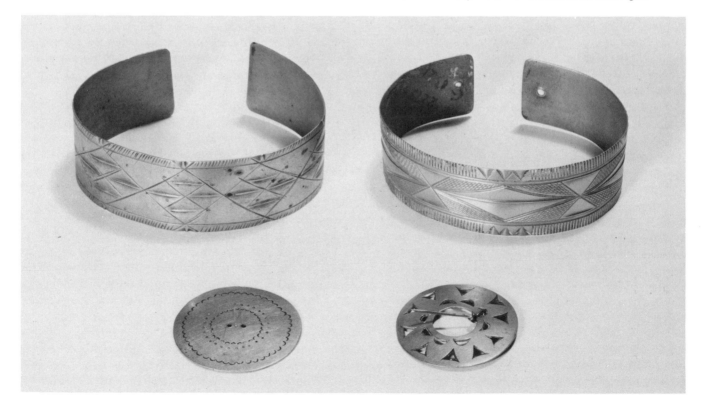

Valley, but it is most plentiful around the Great Lakes. It ripens in the late summer. The Chippewa sowed wild rice in the marshes on the edges of lakes to guarantee a harvest the next year. Wild rice was so important to the Chippewa that they featured it in some of their rituals. It still grows in abundance in the Great Lakes country where Indians today harvest it in the traditional way from their canoes, knocking the grain into the boat, and then spreading it out to dry and parching it over a fire to cure and loosen the husks.

Some plants were used for herbal medicines to cure the sick or wounded. Indians in the Northeast had little sickness before Europeans brought new diseases into their country after A.D. 1500, but some men and women nevertheless had special knowledge of medicinal plants and were widely respected for their ability to cure

▲ A bandolier, or decorative sash, made by a Delaware Indian.

illness and injuries. Modern medicine recognizes and incorporates the curative powers of many of these plants.

As winter brought freezing cold and heavy snow, the people gathered together in the villages. Winter was a time for feasts and ceremonies, and for telling stories on long dark evenings.

▼ Silver brooches and bracelets. European traders often sold silver brooches and bracelets to their Indian customers, but Indians also became skilled silversmiths. Pictured here are two incised silver bracelets from the Winnebago at top, a Potawatomi silver brooch at bottom left, and an Iroquois silver brooch at bottom right.

▲ Portraits by the Swiss artist Karl Bodmer, done in 1833–34, showing the face-painting of two warriors. On the left is Massica, a Sauk; on the right is Wakusasse, a Fox. The Sauk and Fox Indians originally lived around the western Great Lakes.

CLOTHING

The Northeastern woodlands provided the Indians with everything they needed before Europeans arrived. Animal skins provided the material from which the women made the clothes, sewing finely tanned hides with bone or wooden awls and leather thongs. In cold months, men wore a shirt of tanned deerskin, leggings, a loin cloth, which was made of a long piece of deerskin worn between the legs and folded over a belt so it hung down at the front and back, and moccasins, often with a robe around their shoulders. In the summertime, when the weather was hot and humid, they would often wear only moccasins and a loin cloth. Indian women generally wore a deerskin dress that was belted at the waist and reached to the knees, and high moccasins that came above the calf.

Northeastern Indians were fond of decoration. They embroidered their clothes with porcupine quills and, after European traders arrived, with glass beads. Men and women wore necklaces, earrings, and bracelets fashioned from native copper, shells, or materials obtained from Euro-

▲ The small, rounded huts known as wigwams are made from a framework of saplings. Pieces of bark are laid over the framework and sewn together with tough roots, as shown here.

peans. Northeastern Indian men adopted a variety of hairstyles. Some plucked out all their hair except for a scalp-lock; others wore their hair long, often in braids, or in roach style (brushed straight back from the forehead). Men and women in many tribes also tattooed their bodies and faces.

HOMES

Unlike Plains Indians who lived in tepees made of buffalo skins, Indians in the Northeast lived in a variety of houses constructed from wood, birch-bark, and brush. Some, like the Iroquois, Huron, and Abnaki, had longhouses that sheltered several families. These structures were built around a framework of poles with a bark covering and were often about 60 feet long and as much as 20 feet high and wide. A hallway ran down the middle and individual families occupied separate compartments in the longhouse, although they often shared a fireplace with another family. Other tribes lived in conical or rounded huts, made from pieces of birch bark or grass, laid over a structure of saplings and sewed

together with roots. These houses came to be called wigwams, which is the Micmac word for shelter. Northeastern Indians also erected temporary lodgings that were easily dismantled or moved when they were away on hunting trips. Sometimes Indians built a palisade (tall fence of pointed stakes) around the village for defense. After several years of living in the same place, the people would move to another location and build a new village, so that the plants and game in the surrounding area would not be permanently depleted.

EVERYDAY OBJECTS

Using wood, bone, and stone, Indians were able to make tools and weapons: bows and arrows, axes, awls, spears, scrapers, ladles, and pots.

▲ A splint basket made from black ash. When making baskets from splints, thin strips of wood are woven together in various designs. For centuries, Northeastern Indians made baskets and bags by weaving fibers. The use of splints to make baskets seems to have developed after European contact, when Indians began making baskets for sale. Splint baskets became common throughout the Northeast and were made by most tribes.

AN OTTAWA LONGHOUSE

Building a longhouse, as described by Antoine de la Mothe Cadillac in the late 17th century:

As to their huts, they are built like arbors. They drive into the ground very long poles as thick as one's leg and join them to one another by making them curve and bend over at the top; they tie and fasten them together with basswood bark, which they use in the same way as we do our thread and cordage. They then entwine with these large poles crosspieces as thick as one's arm and cover them from top to bottom with the bark of firs and cedars, which they fasten to the poles and the cross-branches; they leave an opening about two feet wide at the ridge, which runs from one end to the other. It is certain that their huts are weatherproof, and no rain whatever gets into them; they are generally one hundred to one hundred and thirty feet long by twenty-four feet wide and twenty high. There is an upper floor on both sides, and each family has its little apartment. There is also a door at each end. Their streets are regular like those of our villages.

W. Vernon Kinietz, *The Indians of the Western Great Lakes, 1615–1760,* University of Michigan Press, Ann Arbor Paperbacks, 1965, p. 242.

▲ The framework for a longhouse was made of poles tied together with leather thongs. The framework was then covered with bark.

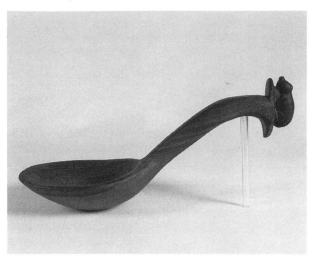

▲ Indian clans adopted animal names and symbols. This spoon, carved by Oneida Richard Chrisjohn, has the emblem of the bear clan carved into it.

They made containers and boxes from birch bark, and often decorated them with elaborate designs of porcupine quills or etched patterns into the bark. Women with nimble fingers twined wood splints, reeds, and sweet grass into baskets, and produced pottery fashioned from clay.

When Europeans arrived with metal goods and woolen clothing, many Indians were eager to obtain these new things. But Northeastern Indians also made things that Europeans were quick to use and copy. The Micmac and Malecite of Nova Scotia made especially beautiful birch-bark canoes, although most of the other tribes built fine canoes also. In the heavily forested regions of the Northeast, paddling a canoe along a river or lake was the easiest and quickest way to travel. Building a canoe took time and skill, but the canoes lasted many years. Men cut the bark in sheets from large white birch trees. They laid the sheets on the ground and then folded them over the wooden frame of the canoe. Taking spruce roots, the sewed the bark together and tied it to the frame. The finished canoe was light and watertight. Some tribes also made dugout canoes from hollowed tree trunks. Indians made paddles from maple, ash, and beech. When Europeans arrived, they immediately recognized that canoes were easy to handle, even when carrying several people and heavy loads, and soon Indians and Europeans alike were paddling the waterways of North America. Europeans also adopted Indian moccasins, toboggans, and snow-

shoes, which were made on a wooden frame, with rawhide thongs intertwined into a mesh. Today's canoes and snowshoes are of the same design as those that Indian craftspeople fashioned hundreds of years ago.

RELIGION AND RITUAL

In many ways, religion and ritual were inseparable from everyday life and nature. Northeastern Indians regarded all living things—humans, animals and plants—as part of the sacred cycle of life. They taught their children to have respect for all living things and believed that all living things had souls. They believed in a great power that permeated all nature and that influenced their destinies. Algonquians called this Manitou; the Iroquoians referred to it as Orenda.

The transition from childhood to adulthood

▲ Making a basket requires skill and patience. Although many people fear that the art of basket making is dying out, some Northeastern Indian women continue to make baskets in the 20th century just as their ancestors did in the old days.

▲ This "strawberry" basket shows the intricate patterns and the high level of skill achieved by Indian basket makers.

animals would go away and leave the people to go hungry. They thought of animals as people with whom they could communicate through thoughts, words, and dreams.

Life was a sacred thing but the creator knew that people had to eat to stay alive, so he allowed them to hunt, and the animals allowed themselves to be hunted. Abnaki storytellers relate how Gluskab tried to change things and learned a valuable lesson. Gluskab believed he had hit upon a great plan to ensure there was always plenty of food for the people. He went to Grandmother Woodchuck and asked her to make him a magic bag. Grandmother Woodchuck plucked the hair from her belly and wove him a magic bag, and to this day woodchucks have no hair on their bellies. Gluskab took the bag and went into the forest. He called to all of the animals of the forest and tricked them into jumping into the bag. He then tied his bag, slung it over his shoulder, and hurried off to show Grandmother Woodchuck, delighted that the people would no longer have to go into the forests and hunt for food. Whenever they were hungry, they could reach into the bag. But when Grandmother Woodchuck looked into the bag and saw deer, caribou, bears, beavers, rabbits, foxes, and all the animals of the world, she turned and scolded Gluskab. If he kept the animals in a bag they would grow sick and die. Soon there would be no animals to feed the people. When animals ran free in the forests they were difficult to hunt, but hunting kept the

was a special time for boys and girls. In many tribes, boys would go off alone without food and water for several days in the hope of seeing a vision in which a guardian spirit, perhaps represented by an animal or a bird, would appear to them. This guardian spirit was believed to give special protection and to guard and guide the young man through life. Men and women alike paid great attention to visions and hoped to share a bond with a special spirit helper who would guide and protect them.

Northeastern Indians revered the cycle of life in their everyday activities as well as in seasonal or annual rituals. Chippewa offered the first grains of wild rice they harvested in thanks to the Great Spirit. Hunters thanked their prey for allowing themselves to be killed so that the people could eat, carefully removed the skins, and treated the bones with respect. If they did not, they believed they offended the spirits and the

▲ A squash rattle. The squash was hollowed out and dried, and then dried corn was placed inside the shell to produce the rattle. Rattles were used in festivals and ceremonies to mark time and accompany singers.

▲ A Huron birch-bark box, embroidered with moose hair and porcupine quills. Scenes of Indian life were popular among buyers of Indian handicrafts in the 19th century.

▲ In addition to making baskets and birch-bark containers, Northeastern Indians also worked in wood. This spoon was carved by an Ottawa Indian.

Abnaki strong and healthy. And so long as the Abnaki hunted only what they needed there would always be animals to feed them and keep their children from going hungry. Gluskab saw his mistake and released the animals, and things were back in their proper balance.

In each season of the year, Indian people held communal festivals and dances to give thanks for the bounties that nature provided and to pray that those bounties would be renewed and continue. The rituals involved dancing, singing, and music on drums and rattles. Indians believed that these ceremonies helped ensure the renewal of life. The Iroquois held their Mid-Winter Festival during a week-long ritual of giving thanks and of renewal and spiritual cleansing. The Iroquois and the Shawnee both celebrated the growth of corn and prayed for a successful harvest in the Green Corn Dance, which they held in the summer.

Rituals were also important in curing the sick. Among the Iroquois, dancers wearing elaborately carved False Face masks performed ceremonies that also helped to cure illnesses. Carved from the trunk of living trees, these masks were be-

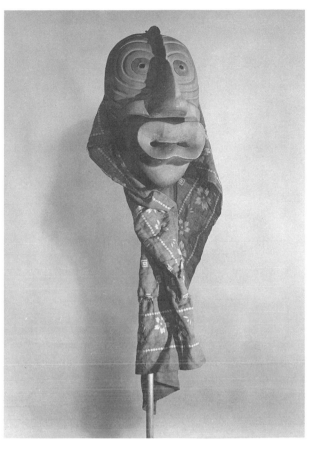

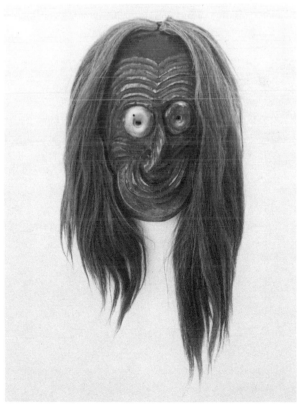

FALSE FACE MASKS

These masks were worn by dancers in the Iroquois False Face Society. Traditionally, the masks were carved from the trunks of living trees. They were believed to hold great power in curing sickness. Many Iroquois people believe that such masks should not be kept in museums for public display but should be returned to the community that made them and the people who appreciate their power and importance.

▲ The Micmac Indians of Nova Scotia produced some of the finest examples of birch-bark and quill work. This trinket box is made from birch bark and decorated with straw and porcupine quills. Each quill is pushed through the bark and bent on the inside to hold it in place.

lieved to be very powerful. Not surprisingly, many Iroquois people today object that some of these masks are kept in museums for display to people who do not appreciate their special significance, and they insist that the masks be returned to the tribes. Among the Chippewa and Ottawa, the Midewewin Society conducted religious ceremonies and preserved traditional knowledge of medicines for curing the sick. Ritual sweatbaths, in which the participants sat in a steam-filled lodge, were another way of curing ailments.

Northeastern Indians lived in a world that was rich in plant and animal life. They understood that people, plants, and animals all lived in a delicate balance, and they took no more than they needed from the land. They knew the land they lived in intimately, and they knew the animals' habits and the plants' special characteristics. When Europeans and white Americans came to live in this country, they were astonished by its natural wealth, but they soon destroyed much of it in their hurry to cut down forests, create farms, hunt the wildlife, and build towns and cities. The Indians of the Northeast were soon catapulted into a time of chaos and radical change.

▲ A fan from the eastern woodlands, probably made by a Huron. The fan is made of feathers, with a handle of bark, and decorated with quillwork.

▲ Iroquois water drums were used on ceremonial occasions. The drum was made by hollowing out a log and covering it with rawhide. The drum could be filled with water to different levels to produce a range of pitches.

DAILY LIVING

THE IMPORTANCE OF WILD RICE

▲ Checking the crop.

▲ Hulling the wild rice by treading on it. Hulling removes the inedible outer husk on the grains of wild rice.

▲ Winnowing the wild rice. The harvester tosses the rice into the air. The wild rice grains fall back into the basket, while the hulls are blown away. Boiled wild rice, sweetened with maple sugar, was a delicacy enjoyed by the Great Lakes Indians.

EVERYDAY OBJECTS

▶ Making a dugout canoe. Dugout canoes were not as maneuverable as the lightweight birch-bark variety and tended to be used on lakes rather than rivers. Dugouts were most common where birch trees did not grow in abundance.

◀ The basket as a work of art. This example was made by a Mohawk.

▼ Everyday household utensils: a bowl and spoons from the Oneida of Wisconsin.

TRADITION AND BELIEF

◄ A corn-husk mask made by Seneca Mattie Young. Corn-husk masks, traditionally made by women, were worn in ceremonies to encourage fertility and a bountiful harvest.

▼ An Iroquois mother holds her child in a cradleboard in this painting by Tuscarora artist Rick Hill. The Iroquois trace descent through the female line, so the child would be of the same clan as his or her mother.

▲ "Creation's Battle," an acrylic painting by Mohawk John Fadden. In the Iroquois creation story the Good and Evil Twins fight a duel in which the Evil Twin is beaten, but the influences of both continue to shape the world.

CHAPTER THREE

WAR AND CHANGE

ortheastern Indian tribes fought one another long before Europeans invaded their homelands. Warriors went to war to gain prestige, to take revenge for slain relatives, to bring back captives, and to defend their villages against attack. Going to war tended to be a summertime activity, and the fighting was usually brief and resulted in few casualties. After Europeans arrived in North America, however, warfare became constant. Indian tribes now found that they had to fight for their very survival, protecting their homelands from invasion by foreign armies and by settlers.

THE FIRST EUROPEANS

Norse sailors from Scandinavia in dragon-headed longships ventured as far west as Newfoundland in about A.D. 1000 They met the native peoples and even tried to establish some settlements, but they did not stay long. By the early 16th century, however, English and French fishermen were making regular trips to the coasts of Newfoundland, Nova Scotia, and Maine, fishing for cod. Some Indians living on the northern coasts may even have already seen their first Europeans by the time Christopher Columbus made his famous voyage from Spain to the New World in 1492.

These pale-faced strangers from the East often wanted to trade with the Indians for furs and other things, and early meetings between Indians and Europeans were usually friendly. But these European sailors marked the beginning of Europe's invasion of America, and their arrival initiated centuries of change and suffering for the Indians of the Northeast.

Following Columbus' voyages, many other European sailors and adventurers sailed across the Atlantic in search of the New World. There were rumors of a rich land called Norumbega in Maine and talk of a passage through America that would take merchants directly to the rich ports of China and the Indies. Some people just wanted to find out what the new land called America was like. Indians in the coastal regions of the continent were soon meeting more and more Europeans.

Among the first of the European explorers was Giovanni da Verrazano from Florence, Italy, who sailed along the coasts of New England in 1524 for the king of France. Verrazano found the Naraganset and other Indian people of southern New England to be friendly and hospitable, but the Indians on the coast of Maine seemed to have met Europeans before and they were hostile and suspicious. Verrazano called them "bad people" and sailed on.

Other famous explorers included the Frenchman Jacques Cartier, who journeyed up the St. Lawrence River in 1535. He found large Indian towns at Stadaconna (Quebec) and at Hochelaga (Montreal). About 70 years later, another Frenchman, Samuel de Champlain, followed in Cartier's footsteps. But where Cartier had found Indian villages and extensive crops, Champlain found abandoned towns and overgrown fields. The Indians living on the St. Lawrence had disappeared, probably killed off by diseases they had caught from earlier European visitors or driven away by warfare. In 1609, Champlain's Indian guides took him across the lake dividing present-day Vermont from New York State, and the Frenchman named it for himself: Lake Champlain. Near present-day Ticonderoga, on the edge of the lake, Champlain and his party clashed with a group of Mohawk Indians. In the ensuing skirmish the Mohawk got their first taste of guns: The Frenchmen shot down several chiefs and put the rest to flight.

About the same time that Champlain was exploring Lake Champlain, Henry Hudson, an Englishman working for the Dutch, was sailing north up the river that became known as the Hudson. Other Englishmen had already sailed along the coasts of Northeastern America. Bartholomew Gosnold visited New England in 1602; George Waymouth was in Maine in 1605.

DISCOVERING THE INDIANS

Early European travel accounts often contained descriptions and illustrations of American Indians. The French explorer Samuel de Champlain used this picture in his book about his journeys, "Voyages and Discoveries," which appeared around 1600. This illustration depicts a girl going to a dance [G], a woman and her child [F], a woman pounding corn [H], and a warrior wearing armor made from wooden slats [E]. Guns soon made such armor obsolete.

"INDIAN KINGS"

While Europeans came to North America in the thousands, some Indians also visited Europe. European, and later American, leaders brought Indian chiefs to their capitals to impress them with their power and to secure their allegiance in wars against foreign rivals. In 1710, for example, four "Indian kings" visited London, where they had an audience with Queen Anne, attended operas and concerts, and aroused great interest among the people and the press. Queen Anne commissioned the Dutch artist John Verelst to paint their portraits. The three Indians shown here with their clan emblems at their feet are Etow Oh Koam, a Mahican chief of the turtle clan, also known as Nicholas; Ho-Nee-Yeath-Taw-No-Row, a Mohawk of the wolf clan, also known as John of Canajoharie, and Sa-Ga-Yeath-Pieth-Tow, or Brant, a Mohawk of the bear clan. Brant was the grandfather of the famous Mohawk war chief Joseph Brant who fought for the British during the American Revolution. All three chiefs have traditional tatoos and wear a mixture of native and European dress. The cloaks they are wearing were given to them as gifts; the Indians returned home from England laden with presents.

In the next 20 years George Popham, Captain John Smith, and Christopher Levett all tried and failed to establish colonies in Maine.

These and other early explorers were soon followed by more and more traders, soldiers, administrators, and settlers. By the 1620s, English Puritans were emigrating to New England in the thousands to build a new society in the New World.

The Indians were puzzled by the first Europeans they met. Some thought that the strangers' large sailing ships were floating islands or huge white birds. European men with pale skins, hairy faces, and strange heavy clothes looked odd to Indians with smooth tanned skins and light clothing. The Indians found the Europeans' language difficult to understand and thought their behavior was rude and aggressive. But they recognized how useful some of the Europeans' trade goods were, and they were eager to trade for these things.

Also, Indians were accustomed to sharing and to treating strangers with hospitality. Squanto, a Patuxet Indian who had already been to Europe (he was kidnapped and later returned), helped the Pilgrims of Plymouth Colony when they first arrived in the New World, and every year in the United States, on the last Thursday in November, modern American families celebrate Thanksgiving, in memory of the time when the Wampanoag Indians shared a meal with the Pilgrims.

Despite these friendly beginnings, however, relations between Indians and Europeans quickly deteriorated. Very often, the two peoples would simply misunderstand one another. At other times, Europeans' actions and demands would wear out their initial welcome. Sailors frequently kidnapped Indians to take back to Europe. Some Indians visited England or France and later returned to their people, but others died, and Indians soon learned that the newcomers could not be trusted. Now, instead of welcoming these strangers with open arms, they regarded them with suspicion and fear. They had good cause to be on their guard. In the centuries that followed, the Europeans and their descendants would de-

INDIANS AND SMALLPOX

In 1634, smallpox struck the Indians of the Connecticut River. Governor William Bradford of Plymouth Colony left this description of its effects.

. . . it pleased God to visit these Indians with a great sickness and such a mortality that of a thousand, above nine and a half hundred of them died, and many of them did rot above the ground for want of burial. . . . The condition of this people was so lamentable and they fell down so generally of this disease as they were in the end not able to help one another, nor not to make a fire nor to fetch a little water to drink, nor any to bury the dead. But would strive as long as they could, and when they could procure no other means to make fire, they would burn the wooden trays and dishes they ate their meat in, and their very bows and arrows. And some would crawl out on all fours to get a little water, and sometimes die by the way and not be able to get in again.

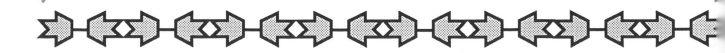

feat the Indians of the Northeast, undermine their way of life, and drive them from their ancestral lands.

NEW DISEASES

The most deadly things that Europeans brought to America were their germs. Diseases such as smallpox, bubonic plague, measles, influenza, cholera, typhus, and others that were common in Europe were unknown in America before Columbus. But when Europeans crossed the Atlantic, they brought their germs with them and contaminated the Indians. Never having been exposed to these diseases before, Indians died in huge numbers and great epidemics carried off thousands and thousands of people throughout America. The first Pilgrims who arrived in New England in 1620 gave thanks to God because they found the country almost entirely empty of its original inhabitants. The reason was that a huge epidemic of smallpox or plague had just killed off most of the Indians in the area.

Some tribes were completely wiped out by disease; others lost 50, 75, or 90 percent of their number as one epidemic after another swept through their country. At a time when Indians in the Northeast needed all their strength to deal with the European invaders, their numbers were being whittled away by the Europeans' diseases. Far more Indians died from the white people's disease than from the white people's bullets.

THE FUR TRADE

European traders brought great changes to Northeastern Indian society. At first, trade worked to the benefit of both parties. Indians gave traders beaver pelts and other furs which were of great value in Europe; traders gave the Indians metal knives, cooking pots, woolen clothing, and blankets, all of which were of great value in Indian country. Traders drove hard bargains to get the best prices, and sometimes the Indians and Europeans misunderstood one another because Indians regarded trading as an exchange of gifts between friends. But on the whole, both parties got something they wanted and neither saw any reason to disrupt the relationship.

In time, however, the fur trade caused tremendous disruption. As Indians obtained more and more manufactured goods from the traders, they stopped practicing some of their traditional crafts. As traders tried to increase their profits, they introduced alcohol into the trade. Sometimes they gave it to Indians as a way of getting them to trade; sometimes they used it to purchase Indian pelts. Many Indians became addicted to rum and other liquors and spent their time hunting for furs with which to buy alcohol. Once they had drunk the alcohol, they had nothing to show for their work. Some traders also used alcohol as a way of getting their Indian customers into debt. They would give Indians alcohol on credit and encourage them to run up large bills; then the traders would demand that the Indians hand over their land to settle their account.

The fur trade also helped to spread diseases through Indian country. Indians regularly traded with other Indians over long distances and they passed European merchandise along from one tribe to another. When they did so, they often transmitted European diseases as well. Thousands of Indian people died from European diseases without ever meeting a European.

Fur traders brought guns into Indian country, and Indians competed with each other to obtain these deadly new weapons. In the old days, Indian tribes who fought each other used stone-headed war clubs, bows and arrows, and spears. Guns changed the ways Indians fought and increased the amount of warfare between tribes. The only way to get guns was to buy them with furs from traders. Indians spent more time hunting and eventually killed off large numbers of beaver and other animals in their own territory. They then began to trespass on their neighbors' territories, but their neighbors were also hunting more than ever before. Clashes occurred, and the tribes became desperate to get guns with which to fight new wars.

These wars were often just small-scale raids in which no tribe won a permanent advantage. Sometimes, however, the wars had dramatic results. In 1649, the Iroquois attacked and smashed the Huron Confederacy in Ontario. The Huron who survived the onslaught scattered. Many joined other tribes, but one group migrated to the area near present-day Detroit, where they made new homes for themselves and became known as the Wyandot. The Chippewa fought for years against their western neighbors the Sioux, slowly edging them out of disputed hunting grounds in the fertile lands of Minnesota.

Indian economies that had worked for centuries by keeping things in balance and harmony were disrupted as more time and effort went into hunting and trapping. Indian men were away from home more often and Indian families often went hungry while their men traveled farther afield in search of pelts to take to the traders. Driven by the need to exchange furs for guns and alcohol, Indian hunters often forgot the old ways when they had taken only what they needed. Animal populations became seriously depleted and when they did so the traders moved on to new areas where the beaver, deer, and otter were still numerous. The Indians who had been pulled into the fur trade as customers, hunters, and trappers had begun to depend on the Europeans for manufactured goods, guns, and alcohol, but now they were left with nothing to trade. They could not fall back on the old ways to support their families because so much of the wildlife had been killed off and so many of the old craft skills forgotten. Many had no choice but to try to find work as laborers for the settlers who moved into their country as the fur traders moved out.

MISSIONARIES

European missionaries also brought important changes. The Christian nations of Europe believed it was their duty to convert to Christianity the native peoples that they met elsewhere in the world. In the Christians' eyes, these people were heathens, whose souls would be lost unless they could be turned into Christians. At this time however, Europe itself was divided between supporters of the Protestant and Catholic religions. In Northeastern America, this meant that French Catholic priests and English Protestant ministers competed with each other to win Indian converts to their own religion.

The most famous English Protestant missionary was John Eliot, who worked among the Indians of Martha's Vineyard and Massachusetts. English Puritans in New England believed that Indians could not become Christians unless they completely abandoned their old ways and lived like English people. They placed their Indian converts in villages known as "Praying Towns." The English also tried to educate Indians in English ways and brought some Indian children into English schools and colleges. Dartmouth College, in Hanover, New Hampshire, was originally established as a college for Indian students. One of its graduates, a Mohegan Indian called Samson Occum, became famous as a missionary.

French Jesuit missionaries generally had more success than their English rivals. Jesuit missionaries such as Father Isaac Jogues and Sebastian

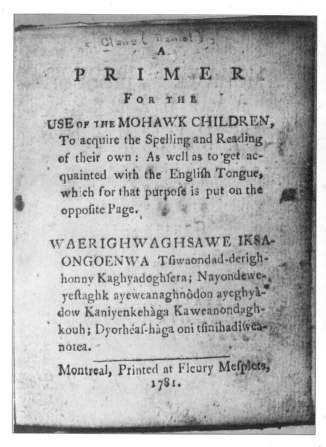

▲ From early times, European missionaries and teachers took it upon themselves to try to educate Indian children in Christianity, reading, writing, and arithmetic. This primer for Mohawk children was printed in both English and Mohawk in 1781.

Rasles often went into Indian country and lived with the Indians as they spread their message. Many Indians found French Catholicism to be less threatening and more appealing than English Puritanism. Black-robed Jesuit missionaries traveled far and wide in Canada and the Northeast, making their homes in Abnaki villages in Maine, in Huron villages in Ontario, and in Seneca longhouses in New York. Other Indians congregated in new French mission villages, such as those on the St. Lawrence River at St. Regis, Caughnawaga, Saint Francis, and Sillery.

Missionaries believed they were doing God's work and saving the Indians from Hell. They thought Indian religion was primitive superstition and tried to destroy it. To the Indians, however, the missionaries often seemed to be just another threat to their way of life. Many Indians became Christians, but others resisted. Sometimes, missionaries were tortured and killed. At other times, Indians ignored them or continued practicing their traditional beliefs and rituals even though they attended church and recited the Lord's Prayer. Today, many Indians in the Northeast are members of Catholic or Protestant churches but still hold on to many of their tribe's traditional religious beliefs.

SETTLERS

European explorers, diseases, traders, and missionaries all weakened the Indians of the Northeast in one way or another. Behind them came waves of settlers who occupied Indian lands and edged off the surviving Indians. Europeans sometimes bought Indian lands; at other times they acquired them by fraud, by violence, or simply by moving on to the lands and defending them against Indian protest. Often, Europeans and Indians made treaties in which the Indians granted the newcomers the right to live on their lands. But there was often misunderstanding. Europeans believed that when they bought the land they were getting complete control of it; many Indians believed that when they sold the land they were simply permitting the newcomers the right to share it with them. When Indians returned to their lands to hunt and fish as usual, the settlers accused them of breaking the treaty and drove them away by force. As the number of settlers increased, so tensions grew between Indians and Europeans. Eventually these tensions erupted into open warfare.

NEW ENGLAND'S FIRST INDIAN WARS

In New England, the Puritans began to expand beyond Massachusetts and pushed into the Connecticut Valley and neighboring areas. The Indian tribes who lived in those regions became resentful and in 1636 war broke out between the Puritans of New England and the Pequot Indians of Connecticut. In 1637, an English army surrounded the main Pequot village on the Mystic River and put it to the torch. As the Indians tried to escape the flames, English soldiers gunned down men, women, and children. The power of the Pequot was broken forever, and English expansion continued.

A few years later, the Dutch destroyed the power of the Indian tribes of the lower Hudson Valley and New York in Governor Kieft's War.

In 1675, a Wampanoag Indian chief called Metacomet led many of the Indian tribes of New England in a desperate war to defend their lands and freedom against the English. The English knew Metacomet as King Philip, and the war became known as King Philip's War. The Indians burned many English settlements and defeated English troops in battle, and it looked for a time as if the Indians might triumph. But Mohawk Indians attacked Metacomet's forces in the west, English numbers and resources took their toll, and Metacomet's followers became divided. In 1676 the tide of war turned in favor of the English. Metacomet was killed and many of the tribes who had fought in the war scattered.

By the end of King Philip's War, the English were firmly established in New England. But the Indians of the Northeast had only just begun to fight and for the next 150 years they continued to wage a bitter struggle to defend their homelands and their freedom.

FRENCH AND INDIAN WARS

By the late 17th century, England and France were in open competition for control of Northeastern North America. The French in Canada were relatively few in numbers, but they had the support of many Indian tribes who, like them, wanted to hold back English expansion. For over 70 years, English and French troops and Indian warriors waged war in the forests of the Northeast. The wars were often sideshows to larger conflicts in Europe, but they dramatically changed the lives of the Indians of the Northeast. War now became almost a way of life for Northeastern Indians.

In King William's War (1689–97), Queen Anne's War (1702–13), and King George's War (1744–48) most of the tribes of the Northeast supported the French. The Iroquois tried for a long time to remain neutral, and some groups actively supported the British, but Indian warriors regularly campaigned with French soldiers, raiding English settlements and carrying off captives. Each of these wars ended inconclusively and it was not until the Seven Years War (1756–63, sometimes called the French and Indian War) that the contest for European dominance in North America was finally settled.

The war began badly for the British when the French and their Indian allies ambushed and destroyed General Edward Braddock's army on the Monongahela River in 1755. But British power

◀▲Europeans often portrayed their Indian enemies as fierce and warlike. These French engravings from the 18th century show Iroquois warriors wielding a war club and scalping a victim.

proved decisive, and after General James Wolfe captured the key city of Quebec at the mouth of the St. Lawrence River in 1759, it was only a matter of time before the French surrendered. By 1763, Britain ruled supreme in Northeastern North America.

The long years of warfare between France and Britain had taken a heavy toll on the Indians of the Northeast. Time and again they had gone to war alongside foreign soldiers, neglected their crops and hunting while away on campaign, and seen their villages attacked and their warriors killed. Now they had to deal with the victorious British redcoats.

PONTIAC

Many Northeastern Indians resented the British victory and hoped the French would return. The British in turn felt little need to treat the Indians with respect. As tensions increased, an Ottawa war chief named Pontiac headed a movement among the tribes of the Great Lakes to drive out the British. The Indians were successful at first and captured many British forts, but Colonel Henry Bouquet soon defeated the tribes and dictated peace terms to them.

One of the requirements of the peace treaty

was that the Indians should return all the captives that they had taken during the recent wars. Taking captives was an old custom among Northeastern Indians. Sometimes they tortured captives, but much more often they adopted them into their families to replace loved ones who had died. These captives enjoyed good treatment, and many wanted to remain with the Indians even when the opportunity arose to return home. When the Shawnee and Delaware Indians delivered their captives to Bouquet, many of the prisoners were heartbroken to have to leave their adopted families.

▶ Joseph Brant, or Thayendanegea (1743–1807), from a painting done by George Romney while the Mohawk was in London in 1776. Brant fought for the British during the Revolution and, at the end of the war, led his people to new homes near Brantford, Ontario, where the Six Nations Reserve is located today.

THE AMERICAN REVOLUTION

In an effort to avoid future Indian conflicts, the British government tried to keep settlers from invading Indian lands. In 1763 King George III issued a proclamation that prohibited trespass on Indian territory west of the Appalachian Mountains. Unfortunately, the king in London was far away from the frontier, and pioneers resented the efforts of the British government to control their movements. Land speculators and Indian agents continued to buy thousands of acres of Indian lands. The government's attempt to restrict such actions was one of the issues that led to the American colonists rebelling against Great Britain in 1775.

When the American Revolution broke out, most Indian tribes in the Northeast tried to remain neutral, thinking this war was none of their business. But the British and the Americans soon competed for their support, and it was not long before Indians were fighting on both sides in the conflict. Most tribes sided with the British: King George and his redcoats seemed to offer the best protection against land-hungry American settlers. But some tribes allied with the Americans. The once-powerful Iroquois Confederacy split as the Oneida and Tuscarora joined the Americans, while the rest supported the British. In some cases Iroquois relatives actually fought each other in battle. The Mohawk warrior Joseph Brant was a loyal supporter of the king and fought in many battles against the Americans, as did Chief Cornplanter of the Seneca.

The American Revolution was a disaster for the Indians of the Northeast. Even those tribes

RETURN OF THE CAPTIVES

William Smith wrote this account of the Indians' delivery of their captives to Colonel Henry Bouquet in 1764:

> Among the children who had been carried off young, and had long lived with the Indians, it is not to be expected that any marks of joy would appear on their being restored to their parents or relatives. Having been accustomed to look upon the Indians as the only connexions they had, having been tenderly treated by them, and speaking their language, it is no wonder that they considered their new state in the light of a captivity, and parted from the savages with tears.
>
> But it must not be denied that there were even some grown persons who shewed an unwillingness to return. The Shawanese were obliged to bind several of their prisoners and force them along to the camp; and some women, who had been delivered up, afterwards found means to escape and run back to the Indian towns. Some, who could not make their escape, clung to their savage acquaintance at parting, and continued many days in bitter lamentations, even refusing sustenance.

William Smith, *Historical Account of Bouquet's Expedition against the Ohio Indians in 1764* Cincinnati: Robert Clarke and Co., 1868, p. 80.

who supported the Americans suffered at their hands. American militiamen murdered Chief Cornstalk of the Shawnee and Chief White Eyes of the Delaware, both of whom wanted peace with the Americans. American troops burned Indian crops and villages, causing hunger and driving the Indians to seek shelter at British posts. General John Sullivan invaded Iroquois country in the summer of 1779, burning some 40 towns and destroying countless crops and orchards. General George Rogers Clarke likewise carried fire and sword to the Shawnee and other tribes farther west. In 1782, American militia slaughtered 90 men, women, and children of the Delaware tribe who had converted to the Moravian faith and, as pacifists, offered no resistance. The Indians and their British allies won some important victories but when Britain and the United States made peace in 1783, they ignored the Indians. Britain granted the United States independence and handed over all the lands south of the Great Lakes as far west as the Mississippi River. The Indians felt they had been thrown to the mercy of their enemies. Some migrated beyond the Mississippi; others, like Joseph Brant's Mohawk, sought refuge in Canada, where their descendants live today on the Six Nations reserve in Ontario.

THE WAR FOR THE OHIO RIVER

After the Revolution, the Americans made a series of treaties with the Indian tribes of the Northeast in which the Americans took large tracts of land. Once the Indians recovered from the shock of their recent defeat, many tribes rallied together and tried to halt the loss of their lands. Joseph Brant played a leading role in the formation of a confederacy that fought to defend the Ohio River as the limit to American expansion. The united tribes won several victories over the Americans. In 1791 a Miami war chief called Little Turtle led the Indians in a stunning victory over General Arthur St. Clair. The Americans lost about 900 men killed and wounded, and this was the worst defeat ever suffered by the United States at the hands of the Indians. But the Americans rebuilt their army, and in 1794 General Anthony Wayne marched into Indian country and crushed the tribes at the Battle of Fallen Timbers. The next year Indian delegates at the Treaty of Greenville gave up most of what is now Ohio to the victorious Americans.

TECUMSEH

Many Indians continued the fight for freedom, however. Some fought against American troops; others fought against American influences and tried to combat spiritual and cultural decline among their people. Beginning around 1800 a Seneca Indian called Handsome Lake began to preach a new religion among the Iroquois. His teachings caught hold among people who were demoralized after the Revolution, and it survives today as the Longhouse Religion of the Iroquois. The Delaware developed a new religious observance that they called the Big House Ceremony. Farther west, a Shawnee Indian called Tenskwatawa also began to preach a new message of hope for Indian people. He became known as the Shawnee Prophet and said that the Great Spirit wanted Indian people to reject all dealings with the Americans.

About the same time, the Prophet's brother, Tecumseh, began to urge the tribes to unite in a new confederacy that would defend what was left of the tribes' homelands. Tecumseh traveled far and wide, even visiting the Creek and Choctaw in the Southeast, and he attracted followers from many tribes, but he was unable to stop American expansion. While Tecumseh was away on one of his trips, Governor William Henry Harrison of Indiana Territory attacked the Prophet's town at Tippecanoe in 1811. Tecumseh joined the British against the Americans during the War of 1812, but he was killed at the Battle of the Thames in Ontario in 1813. Tecumseh's death marked the end of Indian hopes of being able to remain independent east of the Mississippi River. William Harrison's victories over the Indians helped him to win the presidency in 1840, but he died not long after taking office.

REMOVALS TO THE WEST

In the early 19th century, the United States government began a policy of moving the Indians who lived east of the Mississippi to new lands in the west. Many Northeastern Indians migrated of their own accord to avoid war and tensions with the Americans, but others clung to their ancient homelands. American agents negotiated treaties with Indian leaders, using threats, fraud, and other pressures to coerce the Indians into giving up their lands and moving west. Such issues caused divisions among the tribes. For example, the Sauk chief Keokuk negotiated a treaty with

▲ In the first decade of the 19th century, the Shawnee war chief Tecumseh led Indians in a final united effort to halt American expansion onto their lands. In 1810, a meeting at Vincennes between Tecumseh and Governor William Henry Harrison of Indiana Territory broke down and almost resulted in violence.

the Americans in which he ceded tribal lands; his rival Black Hawk resisted selling out to the Americans. When Black Hawk's band refused to abandon their homes, the Americans brutally defeated them in the Black Hawk War in 1832. One member of the Illinois militia in this war, although he saw little action, was the future president Abraham Lincoln.

By the middle of the 19th century, many Northeastern Indians had migrated west of the Mississippi and lived in unfamiliar homes in Kansas, Missouri, and Oklahoma. Others had gone to Canada in search of refuge. Those who remained in the Northeast endured hard times as they struggled to retain their identity and culture in a world where they had once lived prosperous and free. With no political influence and unable to vote, they could do little to prevent further losses of land and they lived in poverty on the edges of new American towns and settlements or on reservations that the government set aside for them on poor land.

In 1887 Congress passed the General Allotment Act, which broke up the reservations into small parcels of land, and many tribes lost much of their land. Abnaki in Maine and Chippewa in Wisconsin lost valuable hunting territories as lumbermen ate into their forests. Deprived of the bulk of their lands, Northeastern Indians could no longer live as hunters and farmers. Many took jobs as laborers or made a bare living making baskets for tourists. American society in the late 19th century viewed Indians as "a vanishing race," doomed to extinction. Politicians and re-

TECUMSEH'S SPEECH

▲ The death of Tecumseh at the Battle of the Thames in 1813 marked the end of his confederacy and dealt a final blow to Indian efforts to stop American expansion east of the Mississippi.

In July 1811, the Shawnee chief, Tecumseh, made this speech to the Choctaw Indians of the Southeast in an effort to win their help in fighting the Americans:

Where today are the Pequot? Where are the Narragansett, the Mohican, the Pocanet, and other powerful tribes of our people? They have vanished before the avarice and oppression of the white man, as snow before the summer sun. . . . Will we let ourselves be destroyed in our turn, without making an effort worthy of our race? Shall we, without a struggle, give up our homes, our lands, bequeathed to us by the Great Spirit? The graves of our dead and everything that is dear and sacred to us? . . . I know you will say with me, Never! Never!

▲ Black Hawk (1767–1838), a Sauk chief who opposed selling tribal lands to the Americans. He fought for the British in the War of 1812 and led his people in the Black Hawk War in 1832. In later life, he dictated his autobiography, which was published.

▲ Keokuk (c. 1783–1848), "the Watchful Fox," was a rival of Black Hawk and an ally of the Americans.

▲ By the 19th century, many Northeastern Indians lived far away from their ancestral homelands. Black Beaver, a Delaware Indian photographed by Alexander Gardner in 1872, was born in Illinois in 1808. He served the United States as an interpreter in negotiations with Plains Indian tribes and earned a reputation as one of the best guides in the country. He died in Oklahoma in 1880.

▲ Ely S. Parker (c. 1825–98), a Seneca chief, served as an officer and aide to General U.S. Grant during the Civil War. He was present at Appomattox on April 9, 1865, and wrote out the terms on which Robert E. Lee surrendered to Grant. After the war, Parker became the first Indian to be appointed Commissioner of Indian Affairs.

formers who showed any sympathy for the Indians' situation believed that the only way to save them from extermination was to teach them to abandon their Indian ways and live like white Americans. Teachers at government schools punished Indian students for speaking their native language.

The descendants of Hiawatha, Pontiac, and Tecumseh were now few in number, scattered and powerless. Most dressed in white people's clothes, attended Christian churches, and avoided drawing attention to their Indian heritage. The future looked bleak as Indians in the Northeast entered the 20th century.

LIVING IN BEAUTY

CLOTHING AND ADORNMENT

▲ The dress of a Wampanoag Indian woman in Massachusetts, as it would have looked at the beginning of the 17th century.

◄ This Indian woman, playing a traditional game at the reconstructed village at Plymouth, Massachusetts, is dressed in the style of the New England Indians at the time of early contact with Europeans.

▼ The artistic traditions of the Oneida Indians have survived into the 20th century, as can be seen in this beautifully embroidered bag from Wisconsin.

▶ Many Northeastern Indians have a made a determined effort to preserve traditional ways of dress. Wisconsin Oneida made the embroidered coat, leggings, and moccasins shown here.

▼ Woodland Indians excelled at beadwork. These examples are from the Oneida Indians of Wisconsin.

TRADITIONAL SHELTERS

▶ This reconstruction of an Indian village near Auburn, New York, displays the sort of longhouse that was typical of Iroquois and Huron villages.

◀ A New England Indian builds the framework for a home at Plymouth Plantation, a reconstruction of the original settlement founded in 1620. The poles of the framework are tied together, not nailed.

▼ A modern reconstruction of a Great Lakes Indian lodging on Mackinack Island, on Lake Michigan.

▲ Wigwams—small, rounded or conical huts—are made by placing pieces of bark over a framework of poles.

CHAPTER FOUR

MODERN LIFE

y the beginning of the 20th century, Indians looked to be on the verge of disappearing from the Northeast. Indian population had sunk to its lowest level ever—a mere 250,000 in the whole country—and the United States government made every effort to break up tribal lands, to destroy tribal culture, and to educate Indian children to think and act like white Americans. As the 21st century approaches, however, Northeastern Indians have increased dramatically in numbers, have survived the efforts to eradicate their cultures, are actively reviving many of their customs, and look certain to preserve their Indian heritage and their tribal identity.

U.S. INDIAN POLICY IN THE 20TH CENTURY

The turnaround in Indian fortunes has not been easy and their struggle is far from over. Throughout the 20th century, Indian people have been subjected to a variety of government policies as Congress changed its mind time and again on whether Indians should be made to assimilate or whether they should be allowed to govern themselves and determine their own destinies.

In 1924 all Indians were made citizens of the

United States. (Many had already become citizens through a variety of ways.) But few Indians enjoyed the full benefits of American citizenship. The Meriam Report, published in 1928, drew public attention to the appalling facts that in most Indian communities life was short, disease was rampant, unemployment was high, education was inadequate, and poverty was common. The report blamed past government policies, which had taken away the Indians' lands and cultures without putting anything useful in their place, and the Bureau of Indian Affairs (BIA), which administered federal Indian policies.

No sooner was the Meriam Report published than the United States fell into the grips of the Great Depression. Now the rest of the country knew what it was like to be out of work, hungry, and in despair. In 1932 the American people elected President Franklin D. Roosevelt to tackle the problems of the economy. Roosevelt promised the American people a "New Deal" and under his guidance Congress passed laws establishing programs to provide vital welfare services as well as to try to get the stagnant economy moving again.

The new Commissioner of Indian Affairs was John Collier. Collier was dedicated to seeing that Indian people also got a new deal, and he tried to give Indian tribes greater powers of self-govern-

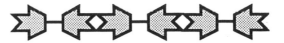
JIM THORPE

Jim (James Francis) Thorpe (1882–1953), a Sauk and Fox/Potawatomi Indian born in Oklahoma, was one of the world's greatest athletes. He is photographed here wearing the football uniform of Carlisle Indian School. Army Captain Richard H. Pratt founded the school at Carlisle Barracks, Pennsylvania, in 1879 and it became a model for other Indian boarding schools. Indian students endured strict discipline, were made to wear white people's clothing, and were punished for speaking their native language. They received basic education in reading, writing, and arithmetic as well as training in vocational and manual labor that was supposed to prepare them for employment in white society. Many Indian students died of tuberculosis and other diseases contracted at schools like Carlisle, and others found little relevance in classes that ignored Indian history and heritage. However, many Indians enjoyed the schools' athletic programs and won achievements in track and field. Jim Thorpe represented the United States in the 1912 Olympic Games and played professional baseball and football. He was named the greatest football star of the half-century in the Associated Press Mid-century poll in 1950.

ment, encourage native arts and crafts, and increase federal funding for Indian students in public schools. Whereas previous governments had tried to destroy Indian ways and make Indians conform to the rest of society, Collier respected Indian cultures and felt it was important to preserve them in 20th-century America. Collier's "Indian New Deal" did not satisfy everyone, Indian or white, but it suggested a new direction in Indian affairs and promised a brighter future for Indian people.

Unfortunately, the promise was not kept. When the United States entered World War II in 1941, the nation turned its energies and attention away from reform and focused on the need to defeat Germany and Japan. As in World War I, the Korean War, and the Vietnam War, Indians enlisted to fight for their country. Many others took jobs in munitions factories and supported the war effort in other ways. When the war was over, they looked forward to greater equality and better treatment in American society. But Indian sol-

▲ American Indians have served in all the United States' wars in this century. Corporal George Miner, a Winnebago Indian from Wisconsin, stands guard in Niederahren, Germany, in 1919, after World War I.

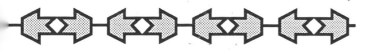

▲ Under John Collier's "Indian New Deal," the United States government encouraged native arts and crafts. In this 1940 photograph, Jesse Cornplanter, a descendant of the famous Seneca chief Cornplanter, makes a ceremonial mask at the Tonawanda reservation in New York.

▲ Kidd Smith, a Seneca carver, at work in the Tonawanda Community House in 1940.

diers who returned home from the war found more hard times awaiting them and a new shift in federal Indian policy.

THE TERMINATION ERA

From 1945 to the early 1960s, the United States government pursued a policy known as termina- tion. During the presidencies of Dwight D. Eisenhower and Harry S. Truman, the govern- ment tried to disband the tribes, cut its ties with them, and end the services it provided to Indi- ans. Without the support of the tribe, individual Indians would become absorbed into American society. The government drew up a list of tribes who it felt had made good progress and who, it felt, were ready to be "terminated." The Menomi- nee of Wisconsin were at the head of the gov- ernment's list. The government abruptly ended

▲ Dan Waupoose, a Menominee Indian, poses wearing a feather headdress during World War II. This is probably a publicity photograph made to show that all Americans supported the war effort, since he is wearing a headdress that is more appropriate for a Plains Indian.

all services to the tribe, which disrupted the tribe's economy and rapidly reduced the Menominee to dire poverty. Under the forceful leadership of Ada Deer, the Menominee fought a long campaign against termination and President Nixon restored them to tribal status in 1973, but they had suffered great damage and their experience served as a warning to other tribes of what termination could mean. Congress also passed a law terminating the Ottawa, Peoria, and Wyandot, and termination even threatened the existence of the Iroquois tribes of New York State.

The 1950s and 1960s were also years of continued encroachment of Indian lands. The building of the St. Lawrence Seaway took away land from the Mohawk Indians living at Akwesasne (St. Regis) on the U.S.–Canadian border near Massena, New York, and at Caughnawaga, outside Montreal, and also brought pollution to their fishing waters. The Tuscarora also lost over 500 acres when the Niagara Power Plant was built to provide power for New York State. The Seneca of western New York suffered the largest loss when the Army Corps of Engineers built Kinzua Dam on the Allegany River, flooding over 9,000 acres of their tribal homelands. The building of the dam clearly violated the Treaty of Canandaigua of 1794, in which the United States promised never to take away or disturb any of the remaining Seneca lands, and the Seneca fought against the dam for many years. But they lost their fight, the dam was built at a cost of $125 million, and about 130 Seneca families had to move away as their homes became flooded forever. Seneca today still remember the Kinzua Dam as a heartbreaking experience, and it demonstrated that there was little protection for Indians' rights.

URBAN INDIANS

As part of the government's policy of termination, many Indians moved from rural to urban areas. The government encouraged Indian individuals and families to leave their tribal homes and relocate in big cities where they would be swallowed up in the mass of society. The government gave the Indians a one-way bus ticket and helped them to find a job and somewhere to live, but then left them to fend for themselves. Many Indian people had a difficult time adjusting to the fast pace and heavy demands of life in the city. Some soon returned home, but others stayed, and new Indian communities grew up within the big cities.

Jobs and other attractions of city life continued to attract Indians, and today about half of all Indians live in urban areas. In the Northeast, there are large Indian communities in cities such as New York, Boston, Montreal, Buffalo, Cleve-land, Detroit, Chicago, Milwaukee, and Minneapolis-St. Paul. Sometimes, as in Chicago, Indians from many tribes live in one area of the city. In other cases, members of one tribe have moved to a particular city; many Micmac today live in Boston. Indians work in all walks of life. The Mohawk, for example, earned a reputation as daring and skillful construction workers in building skyscrapers, bridges, and other high steel projects.

In the cities, Indians have to come to terms with a way of life that is very different from that of their tribal communities. They usually live close together in one section of town. American Indian Centers provide important services, helping people in trouble and giving guidance on how to cope with city life. They also serve as community centers where people come together to meet, to eat, and to enjoy social events. The centers help Indians to preserve their identity and look after Indian interests in a world that can often seem foreign and threatening.

THE 1980 CENSUS

The 1980 Census recorded almost 1.5 million Indians living in the United States. The following table shows the Indian populations of the various states in the Northeast. Many people believe that these figures are inaccurate and that the actual count should be much higher. The recent 1990 Census showed a marked increase over these figures.

Connecticut	4,431	New Hampshire	1,297
Delaware	1,309	New Jersey	8,176
Illinois	15,833	New York	38,117
Indiana	7,681	Ohio	11,986
Maine	4,057	Pennsylvania	9,173
Massachusetts	7,483	Rhode Island	2,872
Michigan	39,702	Vermont	968
Minnesota	34,841	Wisconsin	29,318

RED POWER

As more and more Indians moved to the cities, people from different tribes and backgrounds came together and found that they shared common grievances and concerns. During the late 1960s and early 1970s, when civil rights marches, student protests, and the Vietnam War were tearing America apart, young Indians, angry with the government's policies, began to call for radical changes in the management of Indian affairs. They asserted their rights under the slogan of "Red Power."

The most dramatic events of the Red Power movement took place elsewhere in the United States, particularly in the West, where Indians lived in greater numbers. Nevertheless, Indian activism had important roots in the Northeast and some Northeastern Indians played major roles in the struggle.

The American Indian Movement (AIM) was founded in Minneapolis in 1968 by three Chippewa, Dennis Banks, Clyde Bellecourt, and George Mitchell, to protect Indian people against unfair treatment by white police officers, but the movement soon spread to become national in scope, supporting the Indian fight for freedom in every part of the country. In 1969, Indian students from the San Francisco area took over the Island of Alcatraz (formerly the site of a federal penitentiary that had housed criminals such as Al Capone) and demanded better treatment for Indian people everywhere. One of the leaders of the Indians at Alcatraz was Richard Oakes, an Mohawk Indian who had been born at Akwesasne and who continued to take an active role in the Indian movement until he was shot to death in 1972. Oakes' home community began publication of *Akwesasne Notes*, a newspaper designed to bring news to Indian people, which continues to have national circulation today. Chippewa, Iroquois, and other Northeastern Indians took part in the "Trail of Broken Treaties" in 1972, when Indians from all across the United States marched to Washington, D.C., to protest against government policies and disregard of Indian rights. When the Oglala Sioux and members of AIM took over the village of Wounded Knee in South Dakota in February 1973 and defended it against federal marshals and FBI agents, the Iroquois sent a delegation that included Onondaga chief Oren Lyons, as a demonstration of support for Indian people fighting for their rights and freedom. Mad Bear Anderson, chief of the Tuscarora, was one of several prominent tribal leaders who called on their people to return to traditional ways and revive traditional customs and practices of government.

By the late 1970s, the Red Power movement was fading and many Indians pursued their causes in other ways, but Indian people in the Northeast and throughout the country had sent a clear message to Congress and the nation that they could no longer be ignored and would fight for their rights if necessary.

SELF-DETERMINATION

In 1970 President Richard Nixon delivered a message to Congress in which he declared that, from that time forward, the policy of the United States government toward Indian people would be to encourage Indians to play a more active role in running their own affairs and shaping their own futures. Congress put this policy into law when it passed the Indian Self-Determination and Educational Assistance Act in 1975. Since then, Indians in the Northeast have been working towards the goal of self-determination, but have found it an uphill struggle in the face of economic hardship, cutbacks in government spending and services, limited opportunities, and continuing prejudice and misunderstanding on the part of their white neighbors. Many Indian leaders have pointed out that self-determination means nothing if Indians have no jobs and no income, and if Indian tribes lose their identity, sense of community, and culture. Now the government is talking of a new approach in its relations with Indian tribes. This approach, called the "New Federalism," promises to promote tribal self-government, but many Indians are suspicious of it as just the latest in a never-ending series of shifts in United States Indian policy.

Whatever policies the United States government tries to apply, Indians in the Northeast confront a variety of challenges that test their resilience and their ability to maintain their Indian identity and heritage in the complex and fast-

---

◀ By the late 1960s Indians from the Northeastern United States were becoming active in demanding changes in Indian affairs all across the country. Chippewa Dennis Banks, photographed here with his daughter Tiopa in 1982, was one of the founding members of the American Indian Movement.

changing world of modern America. Some of these challenges are shared by all Indians today, some are unique to Indians in the Northeast.

INDIAN IDENTITY

Unlike most Indian peoples in the western United States, Indians in the Northeast often find that their identity as tribes and even as Indians is questioned. Indians in some areas of the Northeast have been in contact with people of European (and of African) descent for almost 500 years and after generations of intermarriage many of them do not fit the popular stereotype of what Indians should look like. Some people believe that Indians still dress in buckskins, live in tepees, and hunt for a living. Culture, upbringing, and ways of thinking are often more important measures of "Indianness" than are dress and physical appearance. Nevertheless, Indians in the Northeast frequently encounter animosity from non-Indian neighbors who do not understand why there should be special treatment for people who claim to be Indians but who sometimes don't look any different from the rest of the population.

In addition, the United States government does not recognize all the Indian groups in the Northeast as tribes. Some of these groups are small, have married into the surrounding population, and have no treaties with the United States to show that the government recognized them as tribes in the past. Groups like these can ask the federal government to give them formal recognition as an Indian tribe, but the process of applying for recognition takes several years and is very expensive. The Abnaki of Vermont, Nipmuc of Massachusetts, the Ramapo Mountain People of New Jersey, and the Gay Head Wampanoag on Martha's Vineyard are among those who have sought recognition. The controversial nature of the issue of identity was illustrated in 1978 when a jury in Boston decided that the Mashpee Indians of Cape Cod were not a tribe. For people who have grown up thinking of themselves as Indians and believing they were members of a tribe, such things are very confusing. Nevertheless, they remain certain about their own identity as Indians and as tribes, whatever the federal government may say.

LAND CLAIMS

When people of European descent settled in America they took land from the native inhabitants of the continent. Sometimes they obtained

CONGRESS AND TREATIES

In 1790 Congress passed the Indian Trade and Intercourse Act, regulating dealings with the Indian tribes and prohibiting the transfer of Indian lands without congressional approval. This law has given many tribes in the Northeast a basis on which to claim compensation for lands taken illegally from their ancestors. This is the important passage from the law:

And be it enacted and declared, That no sale of lands made by any Indians, or any nation or tribe of Indians within the United States, shall be valid to any person or persons, or to any state, whether having the right of pre-emption to such lands or not, unless the same shall be made and duly executed at some public treaty, held under the authority of the United States.

the land in war; sometimes they bought it from the Indians in treaties. Often, however, they got hold of Indian lands illegally, and in recent years Indians in the Northeast have reached back into history to reassert their claims to lands that their ancestors lost in this way.

In 1790 the United States Congress passed a law known as the Indian Trade and Intercourse Act, which said, among other things, that no sales of Indian land were legal unless they had the approval of Congress. This law, which is still in effect, is the basis on which many Northeastern Indians have tried to regain some of their lands, or seek compensation for the illegal loss of those lands.

The first tribes to win such a law suit were the Penobscot and Passamaquoddy of Maine. They demonstrated that Massachusetts (the state of Maine was not formed until 1820) had taken vast amounts of their lands through treaties that never obtained congressional approval and they claimed the return of almost two-thirds of the state of Maine! In 1980 President Jimmy Carter signed a settlement by which the Indians received over $80 million in compensation and the opportunity to buy back some lands for the tribes. Since then the Penobscot and Passamaquoddy have invested their money to the benefit of the tribes, in developing new businesses and providing jobs and housing.

Other Northeastern tribes have followed the example of the Penobscot and Passamaquoddy. The Naraganset of Rhode Island, the Gay Head Wampanoag, and the Mashantucket Pequot in Connecticut have all won smaller settlements, although the Mashpee Indians were unsuccessful in their claim. The Oneida and Cayuga have also brought suit against New York for the return of lands which the state took from them illegally. Such land claims cause heated arguments. Many non-Indians feel the present landowners should not be held responsible for what other people did 200 years ago, and there are concerns that large-scale returns of land would cause economic chaos. However, the Indians do not demand that property-owners be deprived of their homes, and the cases are usually resolved through some kind of cash settlement. Nevertheless, all tribes recognize that a land is vital to them if they are to keep their communities and cultures intact.

HUNTING AND FISHING

For Indian people, hunting and fishing are more than just sports. They are traditional ways of liv-

MODERN VALUES

Interview with a Penobscot woman from Indian Island, Maine.

I see no conflict at all between having traditional values and living with modern conveniences. I wouldn't want to give up my indoor plumbing, my heating system, and hot and cold running water. That has nothing to do with the values I have. The values you maintain or keep as a guide for your behavior have nothing to do with these material aspects of a culture. This is very important. Anyone can keep traditional values—no matter their physical style of living or how they dress. You can dress in leather clothes but that's not going to make you hold traditional values.

Quoted in *The Wabanakis of Maine and the Maritimes: A Resource Book about Penobscot, Passamaquoddy, Maliseet, Micmac and Abnaki Indians*, Bath, Maine: The American Friends Service Committee, 1989, C-61.

▲ The Iroquois played lacrosse long before Europeans arrived. Today, when Iroquois lacrosse teams travel abroad they carry passports issued by the Iroquois Nation.

ing that are deeply rooted in the people's heritage. Consequently, when Indians made treaties with the United States, they often specifically reserved the right to continue hunting and fishing on the lands they gave up. Other tribes, who never made treaties, continued to hunt and fish in the old ways as non-Indian neighbors edged them off their lands. In recent years, Indian tribes have tried to establish their legal rights to hunt and fish in traditional ways on lands they have lost. Big disputes over fishing rights have taken place on the Pacific Northwest coast in Washington and Oregon, but Indians in the Northeastern United States have also gone to court to prove and defend their rights. In Wisconsin the Chippewa have won the right to hunt, to fish, and to harvest wild rice on lands they ceded to the United States in the 19th century. Smaller tribes like the Abnaki of Vermont have also won the legal right to fish on traditional lands without being regulated by state fish and game laws. These victories not only enable Indian people to continue providing food for their families, they

also show that the tribes possess important rights that the states must respect.

LEGAL STATUS

Indian tribes in the United States have been described as "nations within a nation." This is because they have certain rights that set them apart from other groups in the country and give them special relations with the United States government. Indians are mentioned specifically in the United States Constitution, and over the years they have secured rights through treaties or in court cases. As a result, the United States government has what is called a "trust responsibility" toward Indian tribes and must protect their interests. It has not always done this and tribes have sometimes suffered tragic consequences, as

▲ Traditional crafts such as pottery remain an important part of modern Indian life and culture. Here Onondaga artist Peter B. Jones decorates the rim of a traditional Iroquois pot.

did the Seneca when Kinzua Dam was built.

Many tribes insist on the right to govern themselves and resent any attempt by state and federal governments to impose their laws. They stress that they existed as independent nations long before Europeans came to this country and that they have never given up their right to govern themselves. The Iroquois issued their own declarations of war on Germany in 1917 and 1941, and Iroquois who travel abroad carry passports issued by the Iroquois Nation. Non-Indians sometimes think such actions are unnecessary and disagree with them, but Indian tribes know that constantly asserting their rights and demonstrating their unique status is vital if they are to continue to survive as separate cultures and communities in modern America.

ECONOMIC DEVELOPMENT

Economic development is another key to survival. Many Indians still live in poverty. The standard of living is much lower in most Indian communities than in white American communities, and many people are dependent on the services that the United States government provides. There are few jobs available, and Indians often have to leave home to look for work in the cities. In the 1980s, following the election of President Ronald Reagan, the United States government began to cut back severely on the services it provided for Indians. The tribes had to find ways to build up their economies and attract jobs and income to their communities.

One way has been to run bingo games that offer large prizes and attract hundreds of paying customers to the reservations. The Oneida and the Mohawk of Akwesasne are among the tribes who have tried this. Bingo can inject important income into the tribal economy, which in turn can be put into education, health, housing, and

other important investments. Some people fear that gambling attracts criminals, and controversy over bingo has split some Indian communities.

Other tribes have found other ways of improving their situation. After their land-claims settlement in 1980, the Penobscot of Maine built houses, constructed an ice hockey arena, and opened a factory that manufactures cassettes. The neighboring Passamaquoddy bought a blueberry farm and a cement plant, which they later sold at a good profit. More and more tribes are pursuing business ventures that will help them to exist independently, without relying on government support.

RELIGIOUS FREEDOM AND INDIAN RIGHTS

A century ago, the United States government was committed to crushing Indian religions and destroying the cultures of Indian tribes. Although its policies caused great damage in Indian society, the government failed to achieve its aims. Today, the United States is committed to protecting the rights of Indian people to have their own religious beliefs and the American Indian Religious Freedom Act, passed in 1978, was supposed to do just that. This law, however, has been only partially successful in protecting Indians' right to practice their religions, and the tribes are still fighting to ensure that they can believe and worship how they want without interference or restrictions.

At the same time, many Indian tribes in the Northeast are fighting to secure the return of objects that are of religious or symbolic significance to them. Over the centuries, thousands of Indian bones, baskets, pieces of jewelry, articles of clothing, and other items have been taken by museums and private collectors. Often, these things were stolen from Indian graves. The Indians feel that they should be returned to the tribes from whom they were taken. The Iroquois have for a long time demanded the return of their wampum belts, their ceremonial False Face masks, and the bones of their ancestors. Most museums now agree that Indian bones should be returned to the tribes for proper reburial, and desecration of Indian grave sites is now a punishable offence. The state of New York recently agreed to return wampum belts, held in the State Museum in Albany, to Onondaga, the center of the Iroquois Confederacy where the wampum belts were traditionally kept. Other states also now recognize

that the tribes have a valid claim in wanting important elements of their own history returned to them. Today, many tribes have their own cultural museums in which to preserve and display their heritage.

EDUCATION

The days are over when the United States government openly used education to try to destroy Indian cultures and languages. Nevertheless, Indians today continue to struggle to keep their cultures alive through education. Tribes recognize they must educate their young people in their native languages and customs, to ensure that valuable traditions are passed on from generation to generation. At the same time, they rec-

▲ Modern Indians continue to find inspiration in their heritage. This beautiful clay pot was made by Mohawk potter Sara Smith. The design shows the Iroquois Tree of Peace, a symbol of the Iroquois Confederacy. The branches of the tree offered shelter to all people who wished to join the Iroquois league, and a guardian eagle atop the tree gave warning of danger.

▲ Native Americans today fight for their sovereign status but, as the bound arms on this sculpture by Onondaga Peter B. Jones, entitled "Sovereign Indian," indicate, they continue to be hampered in their efforts.

ognize that a mainstream education is necessary to provide Indian students with the skills and knowledge they need to compete in today's complex and fast-changing world.

In 1969 a Senate subcommittee issued a report called *Indian Education: A National Tragedy–A National Challenge*, which criticized past government policies and recommended that Indian parents be more involved in educating their own children and that schools teach more Indian history, culture, and language. Since then tribes like the Minnesota Chippewa have made great strides in educating their young people. Indian children attending public schools still encounter prejudice and misunderstanding and often find the things they are taught have little relevance to their lives. For instance, the heroes of Northeastern Indian history are Pontiac and Tecumseh, not George Washington and Abraham Lincoln. However, more and more teachers recognize the value of including Indian stories, history, and culture in their classes as a benefit to all students.

More Indian students are now going on to college. Young Indians from the Northeast attend colleges throughout the United States, and Indians from across the country also come to colleges like Dartmouth in New Hampshire and Cornell in New York where they can take courses in Native American Studies. As the 21st century approaches, education is more important than ever in preparing young Indians for success in the modern world *and* for ensuring that they preserve the heritage of their ancestors.

POWWOWS

Powwows are another way of preserving and celebrating Indian culture. Every year, thousands of Indians attend powwows to dance, meet old friends, and make new ones. Dancers compete for prizes but powwows are mainly social gatherings and anyone who wants to may dance. Dancers wear bright and colorful costumes, bedecked in eagle feathers, ribbons, and bells, and they perform to the steady beat of Indian drums. Indian people from all tribes, from all states, and from cities as well as reservations attend powwows. Parents, grandparents, and children all take part. The largest powwows are usually held in the West, but there is a big powwow every year in Chicago, and other powwows are held throughout the Northeast. Powwows are great fun but they are also an important event in which Indian people can display and celebrate their Indian heritage.

LIFE TODAY

Over the years many Indian people have become uprooted from their homes in the Northeast and have migrated to distant parts of the country. For example, the once-powerful and united Six Nations of the Iroquois now live in 17 separate communities scattered across New York, Wisconsin, Oklahoma, Quebec, and Ontario. But, as the United States nears the end of the 20th century, Indians continue to live in the Northeast. After almost 500 hundred years of contact with Europeans and white Americans, the Indians have refused to disappear or to be swallowed up in the rest of society. They have suffered terribly from disease, warfare, loss of lands, disruption of their traditional ways of life, and attacks on their culture. Yet today, the Indian population of the Northeast is rising. Some of the increase is the result of natural growth, but much of it is the result of renewed pride among Indians. For a long time Indian people were made to feel ashamed of their heritage and kept their identity hidden, but now they are proud to be recognized as Indians. The U.S. Census in 1980 recorded a dramatic increase in Indian population in the Northeast; the recent 1990 Census will undoubtedly show another large increase, and even those figures may be too low. Pockets of racism and anti-Indian prejudice still exist, but more and more people now appreciate the importance of the Indian past and the value of a continuing Indian presence in the Northeast. The days are over when Northeastern Indians felt ashamed of their Indianness.

Today many Northeastern Indians live in cities. Most live and work alongside non-Indians. Some go to work in business suits and carry brief cases. But the fact that they drive cars, work in office buildings, eat hamburgers for lunch and watch TV in the evening does not mean that they have stopped being Indians. Like everyone else, Indians in the Northeast have changed with the times, and their ability to change without losing their identity is what has enabled them to survive for hundreds of years. Some Indians, like some non-Indians, know little about their past and care little about their culture. But most are determined to preserve their heritage, and struggle in their daily lives with the challenge of being Indian in modern American society. Their survival into the 21st century will continue to enrich life in the Northeastern United States.

NORTHEASTERN INDIAN LIFE TODAY

PRESERVING A HERITAGE

▶ Many Indian tribes today are making concerted efforts to preserve their past and to encourage traditional crafts. The Seneca-Iroquois Museum on the Allegany Reservation at Salamanca, New York, displays the history of these tribes.

▼ The Turtle Museum near Niagara Falls, New York, presents the history and culture of the tribes in the Iroquois Confederacy in an unusual building shaped like the turtle of Northeastern Indian legend.

▲ Drug and alcohol abuse are serious problems for the Northeastern Indians today. Many reservations, such as this one in Canada, forbid their residents to bring in alcohol and drugs.

▼ Northeastern Indians continue to struggle for their rights today. The tribes' insistence on their sovereign status often brings them into conflict with national and local governments. In the summer of 1990, a dispute over plans to expand a golf course onto Indian burial grounds led to a full-scale confrontation between the Mohawk Indians at Oka and the government of Quebec.

CONFLICTS CONTINUE

◄ Kinzua Dam on the Allegany River in New York. When this dam was built it flooded more than 9,000 acres of Seneca land and forced 130 families to move away.

▼ An armored vehicle of the Canadian army confronts armed and masked Mohawk warriors at the edge of the reservation in Oka.

POWWOWS TODAY

▶ At this powwow in Massachusetts, a dancer dressed in buckskins carries a shield with a turtle design painted on it. The turtle is the traditional symbol of the Northeastern Indians.

◀ Chippewa dancers in elaborate costumes at a powwow in Wisconsin.

▼ Northeastern Indians have preserved, and in some cases revived, many of their festivals and dances. Here, Nanticoke Indians perform the ribbon dance at a powwow in Delaware.

MODERN ARTISTS

◀ A woven mask, made by Onondaga Gail Tremblay.

▼ (Below, Left) A modern sculpture of a snowsnakes player made by Onondaga artist Peter B. Jones in 1989.

▼ (Below, Right) Traditional effigy pot. Influenced by the shapes and designs used by his ancestors, Iroquois artist Pete Jones creates pottery in a traditional style.

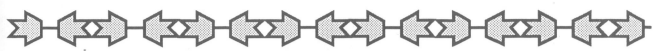

INDEX

PICTURE CREDITS

Atlatl: 94 top; Myer S. Bornstein: 18, 45, 65, 66-67, 93; Brooklyn Museum: 13 bottom, 31, 32 top and bottom, 38 top and bottom, 39 top left, top right, and bottom, 40 top and bottom left; Richard Day: 22 bottom, 23 top and bottom, 24, 70; Delaware State Travel Service: 92 bottom; Joseph Johannets: 19; Kinzua Dam Authority: 91 top; Library of Congress: 3, 15, 16, 30, 50, 51 left, center, and right, 54, 56 left and right, 60, 61, 62, 63, 64 right; Kevin McGee: 20, 21, 22 top; Minnesota Paddy Wild Rice Research Promotional Council: 42, 43; National Archives: 6, 33, 57, 64 left, 74, 75, 76, 77, 78; New York State Department of Economic Development: 17, 71 top, 89 top and bottom; Private collection: 46; Chase Roe: 90 top and bottom, 91 bottom; Eda Rogers: 44 top; Sainte-Marie among the Hurons Foundation: 34 left, 35; Sylvia Schlender: 71 bottom; Schoharie Museum of the Iroquois Indian: 11 top and bottom, 13 top, 26, 27, 34 right, 36 left and right, 37 left and right, 40 bottom right, 47, 48, 84, 85, 86, 87, 94 bottom left and right; Gregory K. Scott: 72, 92 top; James O. Sneddon: 41; UPI/Bettmann: 80; Wisconsin Division of Tourism: 44 bottom, 67 right, 68 left, 68-69.